What Peopl
The Legai _ _ _ Lcosystem

"A leading voice in the world of legal technology, Colin Levy has written a thoughtful, wide-ranging, and invaluable guide to the increasingly important field of legal tech."

David Lat, founder, Above the Law

"This book is an excellent step-by-step guide to all things' legal tech! It's a must-read for anyone interested in remaining competitive in the legal industry."

Julie Savarino, chief client officer, Business Development Inc.

"Colin Levy's book is a ground-breaking exploration of the intersection of law and technology. A testament to his profound insights, this book offers an enlightening exploration of technology's transformative power in the legal industry, from automating routine tasks to pushing the boundaries of innovation. He courageously embraces adaptation, innovation, and technology, challenging the conventional 'This is the way it has always been done' mindset. The insights and lessons, especially the emphasis on collaboration for success and technology's potential to enhance rather than replace legal practice, are critical. His book deftly debunks myths and invites the reader to embrace change with an empathetic approach. It's not just a book; it's an essential guide for every 21st-century legal practitioner seeking to navigate the ever-evolving landscape of law practice. An unmissable read!"

**Robert Hanna, founder & CEO, KC Partners, host of the
Legally Speaking Podcast**

"Whether you're beginning to wrap your arms around the benefits of legal technology or have been through an implementation, Colin's book lifts you to the next level—from the perfectly painted landscape of LegalTech products, companies, and buyers to tips from industry leaders on how technology enhances our careers, organizations, and client value. You will finish this book deeply aware of the challenges in front of the legal industry and the ways technology can help overcome them. The interviews and perspectives Colin brought together provide an incredible foundation every lawyer needs today to grow professionally, increase the value of our services, and drive the industry forward. Because standing still in this market is essentially choosing to fall behind, this book makes sure that won't happen to you."

Chad Aboud, founder, Chad Aboud Consulting

"In the fast-paced legal world, technology is a game-changer that empowers lawyers and transforms client experiences. When utilized effectively, it drastically improves efficiency and innovation in legal services. Colin Levy, a leader in legal tech, has been instrumental in this change through his unwavering commitment to progress. His book, *The Legal Tech Ecosystem: Innovation, Advancement & the Future of Law Practice*, serves as an insightful guide, steering readers through the intricacies of legal technology. It's an indispensable tool for those bold enough to reshape the legal landscape."

Mitch Jackson, 2013 California Litigation Trial Lawyer of the Year

"A timely and much needed survey of the legal tech landscape and how innovation and change are disrupting legal practice."

Bjarne P. Tellman, general counsel, Haleon

"*The Legal Tech Ecosystem: Innovation, Advancement & the Future of Law Practice* embraces the awesome idea that technology can be a trusted partner in the business of law. Imagine a place where algorithms and bots are more reliable than the sun rising in the East and setting in the West. It's this leap of faith that Colin Levy's book encourages us to take, with a persuasive charm that's hard to resist. As you dive deep into its pages, you'll believe in the transformative influence of artificial intelligence, compelling contract management solutions, and the powerful potential of big data. The contributors to Colin's novel deserve a standing ovation for their insightful perspectives and practical solutions that one might call a rallying cry to embrace the future from where we stand today: At the intersection of innovation and institution. Readers will walk away armed with the belief that technology can enhance, not replace, the human touch in the business of law."

Tommie Tavares-Ferreira, head of Legal Operations, Cedar

"Colin brings a unique and exceptional knowledge to all things Legal Operations and Technology. Writing specifically on *The Legal Tech Ecosystem*, Colin provides discernment and wisdom that benefits a wide range of professionals (from new entrants to established veterans). What makes Colin the most impactful is he continually and organically shows up for the greater good. This read is a culmination of all his passion, research, and time given to help others. I hope you feel and appreciate the *malama* (care) and *kokua* (help) Colin joyfully provides. *Mahalo nui loa* for being a reliable pillar in our industry."

Justin Vergara, Corporate and Commercial Solutions @ UnitedLex

"As digital innovation continues to accelerate, keeping current, testing, and onboarding technology solutions is increasingly challenging for legal teams. Developing an understanding of the real work problems those lawyers and clients face and how solutions are evolving from the legal tech ecosystem is key to decreasing onboarding and adoption intervals. Here, Colin S. Levy provides a thoughtful survey of different legal workflows, discussion of the evolution of the current legal tech solutions, and recommendation for continuing evaluation of future technology development. Sprinkled with experiences and stories from other legal tech leaders, *The Legal Tech Ecosystem* is a vital companion for anyone steering firms' innovation and information technologies, business's legal departments, or just interested in technology's impact on the practice of law."

Zack Barnes, director of IP Operations-Fox Factory and legal tech aficionado

"Colin Levy has compiled a wealth of insights from key figures in legal technology—a great starting point for those wishing to delve into the challenges and opportunities presented by technology in legal services. Levy's emphasis on bold experimentation and learning-by-doing encourages readers to embrace change and adapt to the evolving legal landscape."

Mitchell E. Kowalski, author, *The Great Legal Reformation: Notes from the Field*

The Legal Tech
ECOSYSTEM

The Legal Tech
ECOSYSTEM

*Innovation, Advancement
& the Future of Law Practice*

Colin S. Levy

Foreword by Bjarne P. Tellmann

RAMSES HOUSE PUBLISHING LLC
BALTIMORE, MD

The Legal Tech Ecosystem: Innovation, Advancement & the Future of Law Practice
Copyright © 2023 Colin S. Levy (www.colinslevy.com)

Published by Ramses House Publishing LLC, Baltimore, MD
www.publishingforlawyers.com

First Printing, 2023
ISBN 979-8-9856335-0-4 paperback
ISBN 979-8-9856335-1-1 hard cover
ISBN 979-8-9856335-2-8 eBook

Library of Congress Control No.: 2023912653

Notice: The book provides insight on all matters of technology and innovation in the legal industry using interviews of key people in legal technology.

Printed and bound in the United States of America

Colin S. Levy
Weston, MA 02493

To my husband, Jared

You have been and will always remain my rock, my oracle of common sense, and my lighthouse showing the way forward amid the waves and winds of ideas and thoughts in my head.

This project would not have been possible without your love and unwavering support.

Contents

Acknowledgments

A S I REFLECT ON THE JOURNEY OF WRITING THIS BOOK, I am filled with gratitude for several individuals, each of whom has played a crucial role in helping me achieve this long-standing dream of mine.

Thank you to my entire family for instilling in me a love of learning, a love of challenge, and a love for pursuing dreams, and standing with me as I went about achieving those dreams, all while putting up with me and encouraging me when I was at my worst—feeling down-trodden and discouraged.

Thank you especially to my husband, who has always been my confidant, my rock, my sounding board, and my biggest advocate.

Thank you to my friends and colleagues in the legal tech space who have graciously shared their lessons learned, their experiences, and their journeys with me as I went about my own ... and for inspiring me to write this book and not to cease writing and building up the legal tech world.

I am truly incredibly fortunate to have such a wonderful community of people in my life who have stood by me through thick and thin, offering their guidance, their wisdom, and their unwavering belief in me. Your kindness and generosity have meant the world to me, and I am forever grateful for the love and support you have shown me.

Thank you all individually and collectively for everything you have done to help me on this journey. This book is not an accomplishment I, alone, share, but one that each person I have met, spoken to, and learned from shares in as well.

About the Author

COLIN S. LEVY EMBRACES ADAPTATION, INNOVATION, AND technology. He does not accept, "This is the way it has always been done."

Colin is a lawyer, consultant, a sought-after writer, and speaker and has served as the legal leader for several tech companies. In 2022, he was named to the prestigious Fastcase 50 list of legal innovators. Colin is frequently named as a person to follow for learning about legal tech online. His blog was listed as one of the most followed legal tech blogs of 2023.

Colin is the editor of the *Handbook of Legal Tech*, published in 2023 by Globe Law and Business, and is frequently asked to contribute articles and to participate on podcasts on various law outlets, including Above the Law, Law.com, Bloomberg Law News, Artificial

Lawyer, Prism Legal, and others. He is also one of the most widely followed legal tech voices on Twitter and LinkedIn with a digital newsletter that boasts more than 16,000 subscribers.

Throughout his career, Colin has seen technology as a key driver in improving how legal services are performed. Because his career has spanned industries, he has witnessed myriad issues—from a systemic lack of interest in technology to the high cost of legal services barring entry to consumers. Now, his mission is to bridge the gap between the tech world and the legal world, advocating for the ways technology can be a useful tool for the lawyer's tool belt rather than a fear-inducing obstacle to effective legal work.

Colin often interviews leaders in the legal and legal tech spaces. You can find past interviews and a plethora of other content on his website, www.colinslevy.com.

Abbreviations

ABA: American Bar Association

ADR: alternative dispute resolution

AI: artificial intelligence

ATL: Above the Law (news and information website)

CLM: contract lifecycle management

CEO: chief executive officer

CLOC: Corporate Legal Operations Consortium

CPA: certified public accountant

DAO: decentralized autonomous organization

FFLP: Future Framework for Legal Practice

GPT: Generative Pre-Trained

IP: intellectual property

IT: information technology

LPM: legal project management

MADE: Massachusetts Defense for Eviction

MBA: master's degree in business administration

MVP: minimum viable product

NFT: non-fungible token

PhD: Doctor of Philosophy degree

RBS: Royal Bank of Scotland

SaaS: software-as-a-service

UX: user experience

Foreword

"The innovation that is currently underway within the profession will have profound implications for how lawyers work, what they work on, and how legal departments source their needs."

A LOT HAS CHANGED IN THE PAST FEW YEARS, WHICH makes it both compelling and necessary to consider the role that technology and innovation should play within the legal profession.

At the heart of this change lies increased complexity, driven by changes in the macro-economic landscape. These forces are placing growing pressure on legal departments to do "more with less." This dynamic is being driven by four macroeconomic pillars.

The *first* of these is the explosion that has taken place in both the volume and complexity of regulation. In-house teams must ensure their companies remain compliant with a bewildering array of rules that are often inconsistent across—and sometimes even within—markets.

Second, globalization has increased the challenges that legal teams face. Virtually every major legal matter now has cross-border effects. Steps taken by lawyers in one market must be considered for their potential impact elsewhere.

Third, the legal, economic, reputational, and political dimensions of risk are converging. In-house counsel must carefully weigh the non-legal implications of recommended courses of action. The speed and impact of reputational harm in an era of social media are enormous.

Fourth and finally, this increased complexity is coming at a time when corporate profits are declining, which has placed pressure on legal departments to handle growing workloads with fewer resources.

Fortunately, emerging technology and innovation have enabled in-house lawyers to tackle these challenges in surprisingly efficacious ways. Legal technology allows each link in the legal value chain to be handled via a competing array of increasingly efficient solutions that are transforming how we work. These include communications and productivity-enhancing tools, self-help and efficiency-enhancing technologies, and advanced transparency and analytics.

Many legal departments have embraced these solutions already. However, as they are deployed, legal leaders have come to recognize that the technology itself is not enough. To truly capture value, legal departments must "digitally transform"—*i.e.*, radically re-think their organizational structures, processes, and ways of working—*before* they employ new legal technology. Those who have done this have begun to harvest the true value of digital transformation, which lies not in the efficiencies generated, but in the data that can be harvested.

Indeed, data capture is the goal of legal innovation. It can unlock a host of benefits, ranging from better decision-making to insights and analytics. Digital transformation allows legal departments to plug in to their corporations' data and combine business and legal insights in new ways. Legal technology is therefore ultimately not just about generating ad hoc efficiency. Rather, it is about yielding deep, data-driven insights.

The innovation that is currently underway within the profession will have profound implications for how lawyers work, what they work on, and how legal departments source their needs. To truly take advantage of these trends, legal departments must first become more sophisticated in how they allocate internal workload, deliver services, and procure from external partners.

I can think of few better guides for contemplating these trends than Colin S. Levy. A forward-thinking and innovative legal practitioner, Colin has deep, hands-on experience from a diverse array of industries, including publishing, education, technology, and cyber security. He has worked in legal organizations of all sizes, ranging from small start-ups to enormous multi-nationals, focusing his practice all the while on those spaces where business, technology, and the law intersect.

Perhaps most important, Colin has drawn upon his professional experiences to provide thoughtful and impactful public commentary and analysis regarding the changes that are underway in the legal profession. Through his numerous podcast appearances, writings, and other commentary, Colin has emerged as a leading and articulate thinker on all matters involving legal technology and innovation. I have known Colin for a long time and have been consistently impressed with his intellect and deep passion for the legal technology space.

In the future, the most successful lawyers will be those who are agile, flexible, and innovative. Those who can adapt will thrive. The first step in doing so is to acquire insights and knowledge.

This book will provide the reader with exactly what is needed for the journey ahead—a compendium of valuable insights about the changing legal environment, assembled by one of the leaders of the field.

Bjarne P. Tellmann, General Counsel, Haleon

Introduction

"*Being multilingual has allowed me to connect
with others who come from vastly different
backgrounds than mine and learn from them
as they learn from me.*"

AWHILE AGO, I HAD A CONVERSATION WITH THE HEAD of a successful legal tech company. While we have crossed paths many times, we had only occasionally engaged in substantive discussions, and I was eager to change that. As we chatted and updated one another on all that was going on and forthcoming in our respective corners of the legal tech space, we moved on to potential future vacation plans. I mentioned that I had started to learn Spanish to become traditionally multilingual and to better connect with others and their respective cultures—mainly friends of mine who were native Spanish speakers.

My friend then brought up the importance of being multilingual in a different context—the context of conveying important ideas and concepts across business functions. Because of my career journey spanning different roles in various industries and law departments, all led by other people with varying views of what it means to be a lawyer, this idea resonated with me and I immediately remembered all the times I had witnessed how important it was.

What has become a common thread among these varied experiences is that each law department spoke its dialect of the same language—the language of the law. Likewise, other departments also spoke the dialect of their unique world—whether IT, product development, marketing, or finance.

What was also a common thread and commonly problematic was that while fluency in specific dialects was evident, equally evident was the lack of ability to speak in the dialect of other functions. This meant that conveying ideas, concepts, or actions was often challenging and ineffective—and that made collaborating and accomplishing shared goals slow and frustrating.

Not understanding how other functions considered and communicated ideas makes working cross-functionally an often-futile exercise. This, in turn, has spillover effects that can impact effective business operation—for example, when one department struggles to align with another to achieve a goal, like a new marketing initiative, a new product launch or product development, or compliance with a new regulation or law.

The practice of law attracted me because I saw the role of a lawyer as a puzzle-solver, fitting different pieces together. I saw the role of an in-house counsel as being able to build a bridge between various departments since laws and regulations can impact a range of stakeholders and departments. Yet, in practice, this was not always the case. There were times when I felt I was working in one world and other functions were working in their worlds, and nary the different worlds overlapped. It was no surprise when problems arose with various initiatives because of the lack of collaboration.

I recall a time early in my career when I was tasked with reviewing a complex product development agreement. I started to read it and immediately felt lost. There were references to things I had not encountered in my career before—such as A/B test, Cost of Delay framework, and Continuous Integration. I felt I was reading another language. I knew that I needed help to understand what I was reading, so I connected with the business leader of the agreement, and we worked together to understand the deal.

Other lawyers on my team seemed surprised that I engaged the business leader in this task, but I knew that I needed to have someone translate these terms into plain English in order to do my job effectively. I, however, didn't just take the time to learn these business terms; I also took the initiative to educate this individual on the meaning and importance of some of the legal terms I often looked for and negotiated. As a result of our teamwork on this project, I quickly became this individual's go-to legal source. An effective cross-functional relationship was formed that lasted the entire time I was with this company.

As my career further evolved, my passion for legal tech and the relationship between technology and the practice of law and delivery of legal services grew. To succeed in this tech-forward world, I knew I had to learn how to speak the language of business, *e.g.*, numbers and quantitative data. It would make me more valuable to the companies I was a part of. I also needed to translate legalese into English to convey important legal ideas, concepts, and risks to the people who needed to understand them and often act in response to them. This is critical for a lawyer; yet many lawyers seem oblivious to its importance.

While working for a software-as-a-service (SaaS) company, I quickly realized that while I was well-versed in the legal intricacies of a SaaS agreement, I was not well-versed in the company's specific business. I set up meetings with key business leaders, like the enterprise sales leader, the chief financial officer, and the product development lead. It was these conversations, and listening to how they spoke about their work, that helped me understand what these individuals cared about. I was able to learn the language of the business over a few months. In so doing, I was able to convey my concerns or questions using their business language so that they could understand my questions and alleviate the concerns I had.

Being multilingual has benefited me on the professional front and the personal front. Being multilingual has allowed me to connect with others who come from vastly different backgrounds than mine and learn from them as they learn from me. Whether it is a post on social media, a blog article, a webinar, or a live meeting, making ideas accessible regardless of background allows those ideas to spread more quickly and be understood by many.

Take the subject of legal tech. The term has a variety of purported definitions; and to challenge matters further, technology can induce fear in some and confusion in others. To cut through the hype and reduce the confusion, I purposely use plain language and simple terms when I post about elements of the legal tech space to help make the topic more accessible to individuals regardless of their technological fluency.

People are attracted to those who speak in accessible ways, meaning those who discuss and talk about ideas using simple sentences, words, and anecdotes that can help the intended audience or listeners relate to what they are saying and how they are saying it. We cannot assume that even an audience of our peers or colleagues can necessarily relate to or understand all of what we are trying to say. The last thing you want to be in this dynamic and globalized community is an obstacle for others because of how you communicate.

A final aspect of being multilingual is to be authentic—put another way ... others want to feel like they can trust what you are saying. In practice, this means that rather than try to shield who you are from others, use candor and honesty with others.

Suppose you need to say something that might arouse strong emotions in others; acknowledge that before continuing, especially if it directly impacts someone or their job. All too often, we try to shield potential negative impacts of an idea or a suggestion, only to find that when doing so, we create the opposite effect of what we intend. If we can recognize the challenge that is about to be placed on people because of their role or responsibilities, doing so will engender trust and help maintain or even build a bridge from your function to theirs.

Becoming multilingual takes practice. It takes dedication. It takes focus. I am in the middle of my journey, and I have already spent years working toward this goal. If you want to position yourself for lasting success in the world of today and the world of tomorrow, it is never too late to start; but start you must.

Chapter 1

Lawyers and Technology Are Quickly Becoming Inseparable

"It is indisputable that technology is now playing, and will continue to play, a major role in how legal services are performed and delivered."

TECHNOLOGY IS EVERYWHERE.

It is an inherent part of our lives. Our mobile phones have become inextricably linked to each one of us. In fact, the very term "phone" has become a bit of a misnomer because the mobile phone is less of a phone these days than it is a pocket computer.

We live so intimately with technology that it is easy to forget that technology is not the end but a means to an end.

As Marc Lauritsen, president of Capstone Practice Systems and past co-chair of the American Bar Association's eLawyering Task Force, says, "Technology is a tool; innovation is a goal. There are other tools and other goals, but these two are among the most important at this point in history. Sometimes technology catalyzes true innovation; sometimes meaningful innovation opens the door to transformational technology. It's a complicated relationship, like many human ones."

There is no question that technology is dramatically affecting the practice of law. Today, to be an effective lawyer requires not just legal acumen, but business acumen and technological acumen.

The breadth and depth of the players in the legal technology space continue to rapidly grow. Some of the fastest growing spaces include document automation, contract management, and litigation analytics.

In fact, contract management has quickly gained prominence. These tools seek to address four key functions: storage, tracking of key provisions, searching, and reporting. Many of these tools offer alerts that an individual can set to warn stakeholders of key events, such as renewals and expirations of key provisions or entire contracts. These systems also offer ways for users to aggregate data to get a broad view of a particular trend—how many contracts have a certain type of clause, how often a certain type of case heard by a specific judge was settled, and so on.

Each system differs in its ability to handle data and how those data can be input for analysis. Some systems are better suited to small companies while others are better suited to large enterprises.

Related to this technology is contract automation, which is based on the concept of document assembly. Essentially, document assembly consists of a template with blanks for another party to complete and a process in which that party goes through the document and fills in the blanks.

Today's technology has allowed us to move far beyond this simplistic task to create entire documents without having to type a single word. Many of these document assembly programs work with programs likely to be in use already, such as Microsoft Word or Share-Point.

Another type of legal technology is litigation analytics. Litigation analytics draws conclusions that can be acted upon from a defined set of legal data. Typically, the data themselves and the conclusions to be drawn are based on some form of statistical analysis. A prominent company in this space is Lex Machina.

The practice of law is changing quickly. Many people do not understand the interplay between legal tech and law practice (see *Figure 1*). It is up to each one of us—law schools, law students, lawyers, law firms, and in-house law departments—to ensure that we are delivering legal services as optimally as we can, today and in the future. It is indisputable that technology is now playing, and will continue to play, a major role in how legal services are performed and delivered.

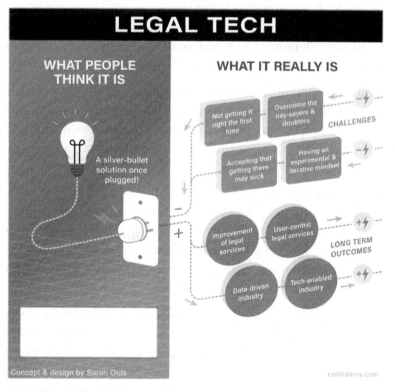

Figure 1: A silver bullet solution ... once plugged in.

Perhaps you are wondering who I am and why I wrote this book. I am a lawyer and a legal technology advocate and guide. I create content that I share on various media, including social media and via my website. I am passionate about learning, about inspiring others, and about supporting and growing the community of those seeking to better align legal services with those in need of those services.

The basis for this book is my blog. The blog started as a means for me to write about what I had learned from speaking to many different thinkers, creators, and teachers within the legal space. Many of these people are quoted in this book. The blog takes a people-first approach, as does this book—meaning that I believe that stories are best told by those who experience the stories.

When I first heard the terms "legal innovation" and "legal technology," I had no idea what they meant. Zero idea. Back in law school, little did I know that I had already used, and was well-versed in, some technological tools used in the practice of law—such as Concordance, Relativity, and Summation. These were leading tools at the time in the electronic discovery (e-discovery) field.

Although I had always felt an attraction to technology, which led to my being part of a tech start-up in high school, it remained foggy how best to engage in this developing passion—considering I had also loved the law with its distinct approach to solving problems and its multidisciplinary nature.

The question facing me was how to learn about legal innovation and legal technology. I decided I'd take a risk and start to network with those working in the space. I had no idea that I would be entering, and eventually becoming embedded in, a world filled with some of the most fascinating, welcoming, and supportive folks I had ever met in my life.

Tunji Williams is one of those folks. He is a dreamer, entrepreneur, a former legal technologist, and an attorney who focused for a time on developing teams and strategies to help revolutionize deal process technology and service delivery for corporate transactions. I asked him what he would say to those who want to get into legal technology. He advised:

"Ask the right questions, and then listen and observe more than you speak. There are a million challenges to be solved in this space. When you take the time to ask practitioners and their stakeholders the right questions, they will lead you to what you need to build. The most powerful and best-loved products are born from a deep and genuine understanding of people and their problems. You gather those critical insights when you humble yourself and listen.

"Be bold and have a bias for action. Unlike legal practice, legal tech entrepreneurship and innovation are not about endless planning and having all the answers. They are about bold, efficient, and focused experimentation. Don't be scared to learn by doing. And remember that every incremental rejection and failure comes with necessary learning.

"Surround yourself with talented and good people. It's hard work building a legal tech company. It's vital to have smart, relentless, and kind people to build alongside you. As smart as you may be, we all have blind spots and weak links in our chain of talents. Great partners will amplify your efforts and make the journey more joyful."

Consider this book a tour guide in your exploration of legal technology. It will not give you specific answers, but it will share stories and lessons from those experienced in the legal tech sphere.

If you are looking for a how-to guide, this is not it. There are other books I can recommend for that purpose.[1] But I hope this guide will

---

[1] Three books that I recommend are *The Simple Guide to Legal Innovation: Basics Every Lawyer Should Know*, by Lucy Bassli; *Successful Innovation Outcomes in Law: A Practical Guide for Law Firms, Law Departments and Other Legal Organizations*, by Dennis Kennedy; and *AI for Lawyers: How Artificial Intelligence Is Adding Value, Amplifying Expertise, and Transforming Careers*, by Noah Waisberg and Alexander Hudek. See the section, "Further Reading," for details.

inspire you to begin your own journey or reignite your desire to explore a fascinating world.

A WORD ABOUT LEGAL OPERATIONS

The legal industry has undergone significant changes in recent years, with the advent of legal technology and the emergence of legal operations as a distinct field. Legal operations and legal technology are closely related and have a symbiotic relationship, as legal technology enables legal operations to be more efficient and effective, while legal operations provides the framework for the implementation and management of legal technology.

Legal operations is the application of business and technical expertise to the legal function and its delivery of legal services. It is this expertise that allows for the legal function to ensure that the right technologies and processes are developed and followed, and it ensures that the legal function serves as an effective business partner to the rest of the business.

A primary focus of the legal operations function is on operations and administration, including, for example, specific things like budgeting, staffing, and process improvement, along with technology-vetting and implementation.

Tom Stephenson, director of legal operations for Credit Karma and a legal operations expert, notes that:

> *"Legal operations is often viewed as corporate architects tasked with running legal like a business through designing, implementing, and managing the systems, processes, and procedures that enable a company to achieve its goals. Critical in navigating our complex legal landscape, legal operations partners with various stakeholders to protect the company's interests while supporting its success."*

Perhaps the most preeminent organization dedicated to legal operations is CLOC, formally known as the Corporate Legal Operations Consortium. CLOC lists 12 key functional areas that legal operations encompasses. These are financial management, business intelligence, training and development, technology, strategic planning, service delivery models, project and program management, practice operations, organization optimization and health, knowledge management, information governance, and firm and vendor management. There are many resources available on legal operations, including many found on the CLOC website.

As for some of the key areas where legal tech and legal operations overlap, six of the more evident areas are data management, e-discovery, contract management, legal research, project management, and process improvement.

a. Data Management

One of the main challenges that companies face when it comes to data is the sheer volume of it. With the explosion of digital information in recent years, organizations are struggling to keep up with the amount of data they are collecting and storing. This is especially true in the legal department, where data are often siloed and difficult to access. Legal technology can be used to collect, store, and analyze large amounts of data, such as e-discovery data or contract data.

Legal operations professionals can then use those data to identify trends and contribute to making strategic decisions pertaining to things like resource allocation and aligning personnel and expertise with business needs. The legal operations function can use data to track the performance of legal teams and service providers, which can help legal departments identify areas for improvement.

b. e-Discovery

With e-discovery, legal technology can be used to automate the process of identifying, collecting, and reviewing electronic documents that are relevant to a legal case. Legal operations professionals can then use this data to identify patterns and trends and make informed decisions. Some legal operations professionals are experts in e-discovery tools, which are digital solutions used to automate many time-consuming aspects of the e-discovery process, including data collection, processing, and review. Legal operations professionals using these solutions can help businesses reduce the expense of e-discovery as well as reduce the opportunity for error or omissions.

c. Contract Management

Legal operations can help with contract management in several ways. It can assist with the creation and negotiation of contracts, ensure compliance with legal and regulatory requirements, and manage the execution and storage of contracts. Additionally, legal operations professionals can provide insights into key contract performance metrics, such as renewal rates and dispute resolution. They can also implement technology solutions, such as contract management software, to streamline the contract management process.

These solutions are often used to automate the process of creating, reviewing, and managing contracts. Legal operations professionals can then use those data to identify patterns and trends in contract language, negotiation strategies, and performance metrics while providing data to the legal function to facilitate better legal strategies and more data-driven decision-making.

d. Legal Research

Legal research is another key space where legal technology and legal operations overlap. There exist digital solutions that can retrieve relevant legal information, identify trends in case law and litigation strategies, and accordingly provide clients with more informed advice in relation to litigating a matter.

Legal operations professionals using legal technologies also can help identify and access relevant legal resources, such as statutes, case law, and regulatory guidance. They can provide support in managing and organizing legal research by creating and maintaining research databases and protocols. They can also help in creating and maintaining legal research training programs for legal teams and other stakeholders. Legal operations can provide both strategic and operational support to help organizations effectively conduct legal research work.

Ultimately, legal operations, at its best, develops and uses both analytics, technology, process improvement, and collaboration to enable the legal function to operate optimally and as a true business partner.

e. Project Management

Legal operations personnel play a key role in project management. Managing projects effectively is essential for ensuring that business plans, tasks, and initiatives are executed as intended and on time. To achieve this requires establishing a flexible yet consistent and transparent project management strategy that, at its core, uses analytics and processes to drive projects forward. Given the dynamics of business, embracing project management is a business imperative and legal operations helps to ensure that remains as such, alongside technological tools and expertise.

f. Process Improvement

Legal operations professionals often seek to identify pain-points in existing processes and inefficiencies, then try to develop better processes to address these bottlenecks and inefficiencies. One way to address these issues is to use legal technology. Legal technology solutions often can automate and streamline these processes, making them both more efficient and more productive.

For example, a legal department may have a manual process for tracking and managing contracts. A legal operations professional may identify this process as time-consuming and prone to errors. They would then develop a process for contract management that is more automated, data-driven, and accurate. Legal technology, such as contract management software, can be implemented to automate the new process, making it easier to track and manage contracts.

The relationship and intersection of legal operations and legal technology continues to evolve. As it evolves, both opportunities and challenges will be presented to those within the legal space. It is quickly becoming evident that legal technology, on its own, cannot resolve some of the more intractable problems that plague the legal industry. Those focused on legal operations are poised to leverage their expertise to help resolve these problems by applying the right process improvement and project management techniques alongside the right technological solutions. Those who wholeheartedly embrace the convergence of legal operations and legal tech will be those best positioned to succeed in the rapidly changing legal landscape.

Chapter 2

Disrupting the Legal Industry*

"Selling products in the legal services industry is not for the faint of heart. Even if the product is useful, effective, and valuable, there is still the challenge of getting it into users' hands."—Daniel Farris

ISRUPTION IN THE LEGAL SERVICES INDUSTRY IS NOW A foregone conclusion. Whether it is the continued rise and growth of alternative legal services providers such as Elevate, encroachment by the four leading accounting firms (the Big Four of PricewaterhouseCoopers, Ernst and Young, Deloitte, and KPMG), or merely the continuing tendency of companies to bring more legal and compliance functions in-house, the business of law is being transformed and new delivery models are being tested.

---

* This chapter was contributed by Daniel Farris and used with permission.

As with any industry disrupted by technology, the legal market is presenting perhaps greater opportunities than ever, as more lawyers, law firms, and clients are embracing and adopting legal technology faster and more readily than ever.

It isn't just lawyers who are taking note. Firm management software company Clio closed a $250 million Series D fundraising effort in 2019, and contract automation provider Ironclad closed a $150 million round in 2022, on a nearly $1 billion post-money valuation (a company's estimated worth after outside financing or capital injections, or both, are added to its balance sheet).

Investment in legal services—and particularly in legal technology—has seen hockey-stick–shaped growth, rocketing up from tens of millions of dollars a decade or so ago to billions of dollars in the past couple of years.

Although it is still unclear how and to what extent the coronavirus (COVID-19) pandemic may have impacted investment in legal technology, it seems certain that investors have viewed the archaic and outdated legal services industry as ripe with promise for new entrants offering a more modern approach.

There is no shortage of hype about the impact new technologies may have on lawyers and the practice of law. For example, the industry is replete with products and services touting the power of automation and artificial intelligence (AI)—although, at best, many of these companies are taking liberties with the definition of AI. That is not to say that some legal technology is not deploying thoughtful, elegant, and powerful algorithms—some products certainly are. Whether that rises to the level of "true AI"—that is, AI that can act on its own initiative, learn autonomously, and distinguish between success and failure and, on its own, change its behavior—is another thing.

And some product categories are becoming saturated—perhaps none more than in the electronic discovery (e-discovery) and contract management markets. Consolidation, or a shakeout, may still loom on the horizon for many nascent legal tech companies.

BEYOND AUTOMATION

Companies that had the foresight to enter the market and release legal technology products and services before, say, 2015, needed to offer little beyond basic automation. Even now, many ordinary legal activities are still done manually, or at least are labor intensive. Simply automating a process was often enough to create a viable product and cause disruption in the market.

The phenomenon is perhaps most apparent in litigation where discovery once kept teams of associates employed with menial tasks. In the early to mid-2000s, for example, document review—the review of documents and materials produced by a party in litigation—generated countless hours of billable time.

A law firm handling a large litigation might receive tens of thousands of pages of documents, often in hard copy. Digitizing and reviewing those documents required the full attention of groups of associates who generated thousands upon thousands of dollars of fee revenue for the firm during their review.

Enter e-discovery software. The process described above was an easy enough one to automate, though e-discovery software providers might take issue with that characterization.

First, scanning documents and using optical character recognition to turn image files into legible text files was the primary goal.

Next came searching, primarily through keywords. More recently, algorithms that test not only for the presence of keywords but also their frequency, proximity, and prominence have been used to turn tens of thousands of documents into a small data set of the most relevant documents in only a few hours.

In so doing, those e-discovery products and services have funneled away millions of dollars of revenue from law firms. Conversely, they have helped to control the costs of litigation and, at least theoretically, streamlined the process required to take a case to trial.

These examples illustrate not only a move toward more sophisticated functionality and features in legal technology, but also a shift in focus. Other examples include contract automation, electronic billing, docketing, and similar high-frequency, low-risk matters that require minimal legal judgment. Today, much of the low-hanging fruit has been picked, but slightly more sophisticated versions of process automation can be found.

Although there is no shortage of products marketed and sold to law firms, there also has been substantial growth in legal tech products and services geared toward clients, both corporations and consumers. Hello Divorce, for example, has created a software-as-a-service (SaaS) tool to prepare and file uncontested divorce forms online. DoNotPay, a mobile app that touts itself as the world's first robot lawyer, was originally founded to contest parking tickets, but the website now asserts that the app can be used to sue anyone.

Increasingly, legal technology solutions claim that they can perform some level of legal reasoning, thereby displacing legal judgment itself. One such solution is Termscout, which uses the combination of data-powered algorithms and human reasoning to provide comparison data about types of agreements and to provide specific answers about what a specific contract or set of contracts says or doesn't say. The development and adoption of sophisticated tools, such as those created by Termscout, demonstrate the increasing sophistication and maturity of legal technology as an alternative to traditional legal services.

CONSOLIDATION AND INVESTMENT

As adoption of legal technology has grown, legal tech companies have begun to steal market share from law firms and other traditional providers of legal services. Many legal experts and industry watchers expect to see consolidation in the legal tech field in the short to middle term. Despite that, new investment into legal technology has grown at an incredible pace, and some of the funding rounds have been eye-popping.

Consider DocuSign, a company best known for its electronic signature product. In 2015, roughly 10 years after raising an initial $4.6 million Series A, DocuSign announced a $233 million financing round on a $3 billion valuation. The company went public in 2018, raising another $543 million.

DocuSign is now a buyer, having acquired SpringCM, a contract and document management company, in 2018 for $220 million, and Seal Software, a contracts analytics company, in 2020 for $188 million.

Another titan, Clio, demonstrates just how focused moneyed interests are on legal technology. Founded in 2007, it took Clio five years to secure a $6 million Series B. Seven years later in the fall of 2019, Clio closed a $250 million Series D.

Meanwhile, more entrenched legal technology providers have embraced acquisition-based growth strategies. Private equity-backed Litera, for example, has been scooping up companies. On January 5, 2021, Litera announced the acquisition of Foundation Software Group, which developed and sells a firm intelligence platform to law firms. This followed three acquisitions in 2020: Allegory Law, a provider of case management SaaS software and a cloud-based litigation platform designed for complex, document-intensive litigation; Bestpractix, a provider of an AI-powered contract drafting platform for law firms and legal departments; and Best Authority, a provider of software to automate the creation of tables of authority.

Although Litera's rate of legal technology acquisitions may be setting the pace for the industry, its total number of acquisitions still cannot rival the 49 firms bought by Thomson Reuters. Whether it is a bellwether product, such as Westlaw or Practical Law, or a new enterprise product, such as Legal Tracker (formerly Serengeti) or Panoramic, Thomson Reuters has certainly acquired (or developed) companies and products that reach nearly every corner of the legal services industry.

There has been a huge amount of recent investment into legal tech companies (see *Figure 2*).

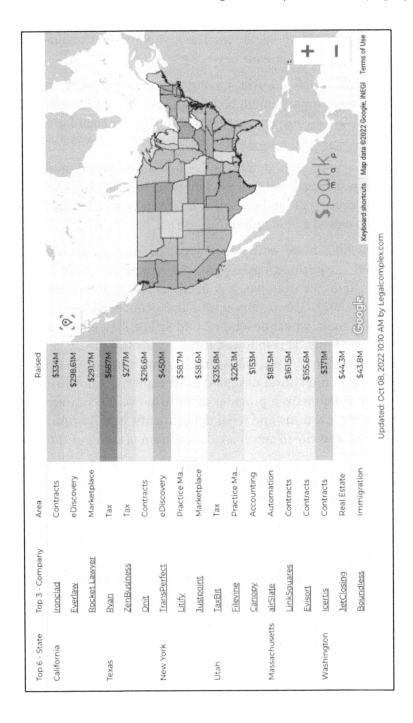

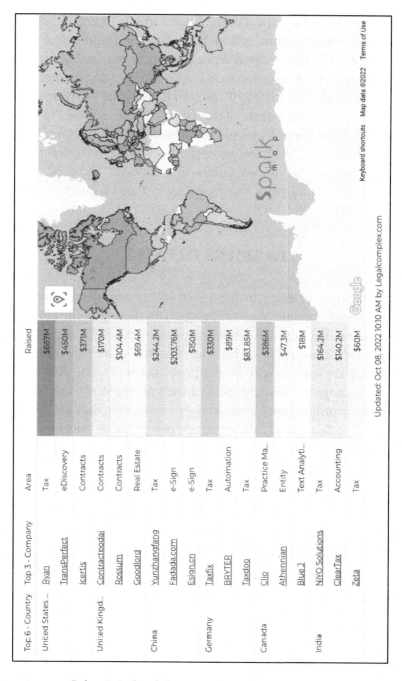

Top 6 - Country	Top 3 - Company	Area	Raised
United States...	Ryan	Tax	$667M
	TransPerfect	eDiscovery	$450M
	Icertis	Contracts	$371M
United Kingd...	Contractpodai	Contracts	$170M
	Rossum	Contracts	$104.4M
	Goodlord	Real Estate	$69.4M
China	Yunzhangfang	Tax	$244.2M
	Fadada.com	e-Sign	$203.76M
	Eisign.cn	e-Sign	$150M
Germany	Taxfix	Tax	$330M
	BRYTER	Automation	$89M
	Taxdoo	Tax	$83.85M
Canada	Clio	Practice Ma...	$386M
	Athennian	Entity	$47.3M
	Blue J	Text Analyti...	$18M
India	NIYO Solutions	Tax	$164.2M
	ClearTax	Accounting	$140.2M
	Zeta	Tax	$60M

Updated: Oct 08, 2022 10:10 AM by Legalcomplex.com

Figure 2 source: Robert J. Ambrogi, "At $1.2 Billion, 2019 Is a Record Year for Legal Tech Investments—And It's Only September, LawSites, September 16, 2019. Reprinted with permission.

It is reasonable to expect both of these trends—consolidation and investment—to continue. Jeffrey Hammes, the former chairman of Kirkland & Ellis who retired from legal practice in 2019, recently joined forces with Adam Gerchen, the co-founder and former CEO of a litigation funder, to raise $200 million in a special-purpose acquisition company. Initial targets of this company are reported to include alternative legal service providers, e-discovery businesses, litigation support providers, and software and technology-enabled services firms providing anti-money laundering services, financial and tax compliance, or enterprise risk management and regulatory compliance support.

BARRIERS TO ENTRY

The barriers to entry in legal technology are high. Lawyers are skeptical, and they are also lemmings. The demographics of the industry mean that decision makers are more commonly older, that is, from generations where technology was not a part of their entire lives. They are less likely to be the heavy users of tech solutions and less likely to have lived and worked with technology as an inherent part of their professional lives. And let's not forget that patchwork of state ethics rules that allude to, but do not explicitly address, the use of technological tools. Such rules create uncertainty and risk around the unauthorized practice of law and privilege issues.

Selling products in the legal services industry is not for the faint of heart. Even if the product is useful, effective, and valuable, there is still the challenge of getting it into users' hands. There are a number of working theories on how to do this effectively.

Some rely on "curriculum" marketing, preparing white papers, speaking, and giving presentations at conferences where face-to-face interaction is possible. In many respects, this sort of relationship marketing is consistent with the way firm lawyers develop business already. It is tried and true in the legal industry. But legal technologies aren't traditional legal products, and that has led many to test other methods.

Social media marketing, for example, can be effective when a firm is trying to reach a generally somewhat diverse audience of in-house lawyers. Good public relations material that highlights use cases or successful implementations can help to validate a product and overcome the fear of being a trailblazer that many lawyers have. And don't forget referral marketing—good old-fashioned word of mouth. Whatever path you choose, do not skimp on the go-to-market strategy—and expect a long, slow, sometimes torturous process for gaining market share.

Difficulties notwithstanding, quite a few experienced legal professionals have taken the chance to make lasting contributions to the field of legal technology. For some, the motivation may have been to reduce legal drudgery (and expense), as the e-discovery products do; others looked to broader goals.

One person I spoke with—Mark Deuitch, the founder of PeopleClaim and RHUbarb—brought up the fact that, by some estimates, more than 80 percent of Americans "are effectively disenfranchised from civil justice because they cannot afford the time and money costs of court. In many cases, they can't even find representation unless their case can become part of a class action or be embellished to a higher potential payout. Yet an accessible and inclusive legal system is vital to any democracy."

Larry Bridgesmith, adjunct professor of law at Vanderbilt University Law School, noted that roughly "80 percent of potential legal clients in the United States (both individuals and businesses) 'go it alone' when they have a need for legal representation. Billable-hour pricing and traditional legal business models will not bridge the gap. Only massive innovation in legal service delivery can meet these systemic needs. Legal technology is a set of tools that can assist."

Mark A. Cohen, chief executive officer of Legal Mosaic and executive chairman of the Digital Legal Exchange, summed it up this way:

> *"Technology is one of three pillars that supports legal delivery; the other two are legal and business expertise. Technology is as much an element of legal delivery as differentiated practice skills and judgment, and it's more pervasive."*

But being a pervasive technology is one thing—being a technology that is used effectively is another. For Cat Moon, there was never an issue with using technology to purpose. Moon is the director of innovation design in the Program on Law and Innovation, director of the PoLI Institute, and lecturer in law at Vanderbilt Law School. In 2006, Moon opened a boutique law firm with two other women. She recalled that at the time:

> *"We were bootstrapping and all of us were coming out of firms with lots of cushy support—assistants, fancy copiers, sophisticated billing software, and so on. Realizing pretty quickly that we weren't financially capable of simply recreating what we'd left—and what a blessing this was—I became the self-appointed tech expert for the firm. I simply had to figure it all out, so we could open our doors and serve clients.*

> *"We were in the cloud before cloud-based practice management existed. We were paperless from almost day one. My practice was 98 percent flat fee. I started using Agile project management in 2009 and have been interested since that time in building an effective tool for Agile legal workflow management.*

> *"So, I've come to this place where I'm almost not very interested in technology; I'm much more interested in the problems technology can help us solve. People don't focus on the problems enough. The technology I'm most interested in building is focused more on people with legal problems and less on lawyers. I want to build solutions that are about solving problems, not about who is solving problems."*

Bjarne P. Tellmann, now general counsel of the health solutions company, Haleon, and former senior vice president and general counsel at GSK Consumer Healthcare, echoed Moon's call to focus on problems:

"First, focus on what the problem is before focusing on the technology. Many are just seduced by technology and deploy it, but then realize it is not solving the problem. It is crucial to focus on the process that has the problem you want to solve. Once you understand how each part of the process works, then and only then can you determine how technology can solve that problem.

"Second, consider the simple technologies we have already. We too easily can get captivated by fancy new technology and forget the power that more basic technology has to offer.

"Third, remember that there is a gap between the theoretical value of technology and the true benefits that technology can yield. We too often discount the fact that, when you put a new technology in place, you are asking people to change their behavior. That, in turn, is an emotional request. You need to factor this into any decision about using a new piece of technology."

The shiny, gee-whiz quality of fancy new technology may be responsible for what Ron Friedmann, an expert in law practice management, contract management, e-discovery, and other aspects of technology for lawyers, calls "the magic button syndrome":

"From the earliest days of PCs, many lawyers have said, in so many words, 'I pressed the button, and nothing happened.' They think the technology works by itself, that they do not need to do anything differently to gain its benefit.

"Even 30 years ago, legal technology offered lawyers powerful practice benefits. That's even truer today. The difference is that lawyers today are more accustomed to ever-changing apps and websites; they accept software changes more readily. Nonetheless, adoption and integration of new ways of working does not happen automati-

cally. Any significant change in how lawyers work requires systematic change management."

Legal technology is not just a new software program that can be seamlessly (well, almost) added to an earlier version; it is systematic change. Legal expertise remains a key component of the legal profession, but it is not enough. Technology has made inroads and continues to make inroads into the legal industry, just as it has in other industries. Emblematic of this is the fact that 40 U.S. states, so far, have adopted some form of a duty of technology competence—that is, all lawyers licensed and practicing in a state that has adopted the duty must be aware of technology and its uses within the practice of law.[2] The duty of technology competence does not explicitly require that lawyers be well-versed in technological tools or even be tech-savvy. However, to fulfill the duty, practically, it does require that one develop an awareness of tools that can help the lawyer best meet the needs of the clients the lawyer seeks to help.

Additionally, clients are growing more sophisticated in many ways; they expect technology to be used in the delivery of legal services. Technology can help individuals with limited finances to access legal help at far lower cost than would usually be the case. This is having, and will continue to have, far-reaching impact on the ongoing evolution of the legal industry and its ability to meet the needs of consumers of legal services.

GENERATIVE ARTIFICIAL INTELLIGENCE

I would be remiss if I didn't address a transformative advance in the AI space, perhaps best exemplified by ChatGPT. When I asked ChatGPT to explain what it was, it said the following:

"I am an AI language model created by OpenAI, called ChatGPT. I have been trained on a vast amount of text data and can answer a wide range of questions, provide information, and even generate

---

[2] Robert J. Ambrogi, "Another State Adopts Duty of Technology Competence for Lawyers, Bringing Total to 40," LawSites, March 24, 2022.

text on various topics. I am designed to assist users with concise and accurate answers to their inquiries, and I am capable of having conversations with users to provide the best possible response. I am constantly learning and updating my knowledge to stay current and provide the most up-to-date information. My goal is to make information accessible and provide users with a quick and easy way to find the answers they're looking for."

ChatGPT has generated a lot of attention given its remarkable interactivity and innate ability to respond to requests quickly—and in plain and simple language. Yet ChatGPT is but one of many examples of what is called Generative Artificial Intelligence. Generative AI is a blanket term used to describe any form of AI model that creates content such as imagery, video, text, audio, or even code.

Unlike other AI models, Generative AI creates new outputs based on data that the model has been trained on. That is what makes Generative AI exciting because unlike other types of AI, Generative AI models create new content, and that content can take many forms. While this is not a book on AI, some context for Generative AI is useful here. Generative AI uses a form of deep learning that, itself, is a subset of machine learning to create this new content.

While the content that gets created can vary, Generative AI has some common characteristics regardless of the content that gets created. Before I describe what those are, let's touch upon AI that is not generative. AI that is not generative is called discriminating artificial intelligence—discriminating because its purpose is to decide, *e.g.,* provide a judgment based on given inputs whether a contract contains a keyword or a critical clause. The AI model is trained to make these decisions based on provided parameters.

Generative AI models typically take one of several forms. Two of the forms more commonly used by everyday people are either a visual generating tool that can create some type of media—*e.g.,* video, audio, or both—or a text-generating model (also called a Generative Pre-Trained model or GPT for short). The content that is created can then serve as a useful starting point for artists, musicians, and writers for brainstorming, outlining, and exploration. Additionally, these applications can create things quickly and in larger quantities than a human can. What could otherwise be time-consuming, repetitive, and costly tasks can now be done efficiently.

There are also some definite risks that come with using Generative AI. One such risk is bias. A biased set of data will also make the model biased. Such bias may be hard to detect at first if the person compiling the data is unaware of a bias within the data because they, themselves, are biased and do not recognize their bias.

What also contributes to bias is the quality and scope of the data sets used to train the models. If those data are limited, inaccurate, or incomplete, the model will produce outputs that are also biased, limited, or inaccurate. A Generative AI model requires an enormous amount of data, some of which could become outdated quickly.

A final risk that comes with using Generative AI is that as more data is provided to it, its outputs can be unpredictable, hard to control, and sometimes even fail to meet what a user expects of it.

AI is making rapid advancements and these advancements are the harbinger of more changes to come. The rise of sophisticated large language models such as GPT-4 represents a major advancement in the ability for technology to be used to complete complex research and writing projects.

Consider litigation as one space where AI can make a tremendous impact. From researching caselaw and drawing out trends, analyses, and winning arguments in previously used legal briefs to extracting key datapoints from troves of documents produced during the discovery phase of a litigation matter, technology can perform tasks that would take hours, days, even weeks or months for humans to complete by themselves.

AI solutions can also produce first drafts of briefs, anticipate potential opposing counsel arguments, and even predict the probability of a winning argument. Casetext, for example, has an AI-based tool called CoCounsel, which answers inquiries traditionally asked of new lawyers about a case or area of law. Many more such tools are poised to be released with increasingly sophisticated capabilities.

In the contract management area, AI tools leveraging machine-learning and natural-language-processing algorithms can assist with reviewing contracts for key terms or risks, interpret contract terms, and even predict potential risks based on historical data. Such tools can assist in helping draft alternative clauses when an agreement is being negotiated or identify trends or patterns with a series of contract negotiations or contractual sales cycles.

Additionally, and importantly, AI tools have tremendous potential to make accessing legal services cheaper and easier by providing consumers of legal services with access to self-service tools and documents without needing to engage a costly lawyer or pursue costly litigation. Disputes can now be resolved online without needing to set aside time to go to court. Companies, like SixFifty and Gavel, allow for individuals, startups, and smaller firms to create and access resources to succeed and establish themselves at a much lower expense and far faster than could be done historically.

Yet, to fully realize the benefits of using AI requires awareness and proficiency in using these tools, including knowing how to ask the right questions to get the right answers or information needed. Additionally, as technologies grow in power and abilities, the ethics around proper use of such tools remain woefully underdeveloped. More work is needed to provide frameworks around the use of such tools.

Law firms and law schools should update their curricula to incorporate technological awareness, proficiency, and ethics to help ensure their employees and graduates are positioned to thrive in a world increasingly reliant on and driven by technology.

Given that context is of supreme importance in human interaction combined with an inherent moral compass and emotional intelligence, AI tools are set to continue to be just tools. Thus, while it is critical to recognize the profound impact of AI on the legal sector, it would be erroneous to understate the enduring importance of human contributions in the practice of law.

Stay tuned!

Chapter 3

What Is Legal Technology?

"Legal technology is about changing what work lawyers do and how they do it, with the goal of helping the profession be ever more client- and consumer-focused."

THE LEGAL PROFESSION IS OFTEN PORTRAYED ON TV AND in movies as a monolithic, predictable, and consistent industry. It is also portrayed as one with clear winners and losers. These portrayals may make for good TV, but they are not reality. I learned this early, while working as a technical litigation support analyst—a fancy term for an information technology (IT) paralegal—for a big firm in New York City before I went to law school. At the firm, I performed mundane and repetitive tasks for long periods of time, subject to the changing whims and demands of temperamental firm partners. At the same time, I was using technology to do this work, using electronic discovery (e-discovery) tools as well as Microsoft Word and Excel.

Once I began my career as a lawyer, it seemed to me that technology could play a bigger role in how law was practiced and how legal services were delivered. I wanted to learn more about legal technology. I contacted many individuals connected to the field—authors, speakers, lawyers, businesspeople, and others—and asked them about their legal tech work. I surmised two things: (1) people's lived experiences play an important role in their take on technology, and (2) each day, legal technology is becoming increasingly important to the legal world and ever more integral to how legal services are performed and delivered to clients.

One of the people I spoke with was Dennis Kennedy, who is well known for promoting innovation and the use of technology in law practice. I asked him how he would differentiate technology from legal technology, and if such a differentiation makes sense. Kennedy had several thoughts:

> *"In many cases, the differentiation doesn't make a lot of sense. Practically speaking, legal technology means any technology used by legal service providers, and that's not all that helpful as a definition. There's standard technology used, say, in a law office, that would be used by any business. There is practice-specific or practice-related technology that legal professionals use internally to perform their legal services. There is also practice-specific or practice-related technology that legal professionals use externally with others to perform their legal services. And then there is technology that legal service providers use to deliver legal services to clients, the public, or other external end users.*

> *"I co-wrote a book with Tom Mighell called* The Lawyer's Guide to Collaboration Tools and Technologies, *so it shouldn't surprise anyone what areas interest me most. We are also seeing a growing use of the terms 'legal tech' and 'law tech,' which can be useful among*

insiders, but to most people are very confusing. If we can be precise about how we use terms, the differentiation probably still makes sense; but technology is everywhere, and the legal industry is already using many standard technology tools."

Technology is a set of tools, and its power lies with those who use it. Many of us already use legal technology, even if we do not realize it and would express reluctance to use it if asked in those terms. Microsoft Word? Google Docs? Those can be legal technology tools. We also may not be using these programs to the fullest extent possible. Microsoft Word, for example, has many useful features that most users aren't familiar with but probably should be.

Kennedy also has some words for lawyers who are reluctant to use legal technology:

"My usual sermon on technology is that lawyers are trained to learn new things and be lifelong learners. If you can learn esoteric areas of law, then technologies, at least a few that can be relevant and helpful to you and your clients, should be learnable, too. I enjoy telling people that I was an English major in college. My friends joke about my obsession with the 'jobs to be done' theory these days and how I like to say, 'What are you hiring X technology to do for you?'

"The fact is that technology makes sense in a context and as a tool to accomplish a job that you need to get done. If you can focus on that question and not be intimidated by capital-T Technology and its immensity, any lawyer can make big strides in improving their practice and client service with technology. I've talked to many lawyers over the years who never thought they'd understand or use technology, but have successfully improved their practices, their client services, and their lives by using technology to apply creativity pragmatically."

I also spoke with Jordan Furlong, a leading analyst of the global legal market, a forecaster of its future, and a thought leader in legal innovation. He has spoken to a variety of law firms and lawyers' organizations, to legal regulators, and to many others throughout North America, Europe, and Australia. The author of *Law Is a Buyer's Market: Building a Client-First Law Firm,* Furlong is:

"hard-pressed to see any way in which technology and analytics could be a hindrance to the evolution of law practice. They're just tools, after all—means and methods by which a provider can amplify its productivity and enhance its effectiveness. You're free not to use any tool that's presented to you, so long as you're prepared to compete with someone else who does—and who magically seems to increase profit margins or market share by doing so.

"Too many lawyers roll their eyes when the subject of technology comes up. That speaks to lawyer technophobia, which is widespread. But in fairness, it also speaks to the legal tech industry's generally poor framing of technological advances—another expensive upgrade, another round of training, another system that doesn't work the way we were told it would. Lawyer negativity toward technology is not entirely unearned.

"But here's the thing: Law firms appear to be the only places where legal technology and analytics aren't having an impact. In-house law departments, corporate procurement and legal operations, legal start-ups, Big Four accounting firms—everyone else seems to be doing just fine adopting and implementing legal tech. Is the tool the problem? Or is it the people to whom the tool has been offered?"

When I speak about legal technology, I start by talking about what my audience is already using before moving on to more advanced or complex technologies. It helps to connect the tools people frequently work with and how they could be using them better, which would allow them to work more productively with the idea of new tools. Starting with tools that are already in use serves to help demystify technology, which can be helpful.

Many who discuss technology on social media immediately turn to imagery of robots and talk about technology "coming after" people or robots seeking to "replace" people. Is that the purpose of technology—to come after you and to replace you? No, that is not its purpose.

A common misunderstanding is that legal technology and legal innovation are the same thing. They are not the same thing. They also mean different things to different people.

WHAT LEGAL TECHNOLOGY IS NOT

Now for some good, old-fashioned myth busting.

Myth Number 1. Legal technology is AI.

No. Certain areas of legal technology employ elements of AI, but the two are different. Understandably, a lot of companies in the legal tech space use "artificial intelligence" to market their products and services, but genuine AI—which we may or may not have yet, depending on its definition—is more complicated.

Myth Number 2. Legal technology is about robots.

No. It may be cool to watch robots jumping, stacking boxes, cleaning, or organizing, but legal technology is not about developing automated systems to do everything that a lawyer does. Legal technology is also not about replacing lawyers with technology. Legal technology is about changing what work lawyers do and how they do it, with the goal of helping the profession be ever more client- and consumer-focused.

Myth Number 3. Legal technology is a panacea, and its adoption will resolve all your problems.

No. Legal technology is just one set of tools that should be in every lawyer's toolbox. However, it will not solve all your problems. It may not even solve all of one existing problem. What legal technology can do is improve processes, facilitate better collaboration, and reduce the time spent on routine tasks, making the lawyer's time more productive. For example, think about a scenario where a lawyer can either spend time reviewing a nondisclosure agreement of a kind that he or she has reviewed hundreds of times before, or can spend time on a high-risk, high-reward deal worth tens of thousands of dollars. Legal technology can help automate the review of the agreement and release the lawyer to focus on that high-value deal.

Myth Number 4. Legal technology is only suited for large legal departments or for large law firms.

No. There are many tools, some of which are referred to later in this book, that are widely used by small and solo-practitioner firms and relatively small legal departments. There certainly are expensive legal tech tools, but there are also many that offer far more reasonable pricing and more tailored services and products.

Myth Number 5. Legal technology is the sole driver of change within the legal industry.

No. Although legal technology is one driver of change, the buyers of legal services have changed (and are still changing) what they want to receive from the legal industry. Instead of a monolithic industry in which the practice of law and the delivery of legal services are effectively the same thing, the industry is now reckoning with the disaggregation of the two. Data-driven decision-making, and the hiring of professionals who have not just legal skills but skills in process building, project management, and technology (perhaps along with high business acumen), are prompting this ongoing disaggregation.

Among the results are new business models and new ways of delivering legal services.

Still, perhaps not unusual in a field where so many are so uncertain about its benefits, myths about legal technology persist. Bill Henderson is a long-time educator and leader in innovative legal education. When I asked him back in 2019 what he thought was the most persistent myth about legal technology, he said:

> *"[It's the myth that] the benefits of technology can be obtained by just buying the technology. One of the most sophisticated and tech-savvy legal professionals I know is Steve Harmon, who used to run legal operations at Cisco Systems Inc. and is now general counsel at Elevate. Steve used to tell his team, 'No new golf clubs,' which conveyed that the gains needed were the hard stuff of designing good processes and training your people to use them. Technology (the new golf clubs) comes last. This takes us back to working examples. We need good working systems sometimes in the legal ecosystem—Microsoft and Cisco would be logical candidates as visionary customers of some leading legal tech companies—which could serve as a kind of model home for the rest of us to tour."*

WHAT LEGAL TECHNOLOGY IS FOR

Legal technology is here to help attorneys spend more time on tasks that carry relatively high risk and require substantive legal input and less time spent on repetitive, time-consuming, standardizable tasks. For example, process automation technologies have simplified and sped up tasks that lawyers used to spend time on in discovery—at first, by using scanning and keyword searches, and more recently, by using algorithms that test keyword frequency, prominence, and proximity. Contract review, billing, and docketing—high-frequency, low-risk tasks requiring minimal legal judgment—have joined discovery in being automated.

Much of the current focus of the legal technology space remains on automation—on the automated review and negotiation of agreements, for example. Companies such as BlackBoiler, Juro, and Lawgeex offer products to help attorneys with these tasks.

Technology also can be used to make the practice of law more accessible and understandable to those not trained in the practice of law—one could say "humanizing" the practice of law. A foremost voice in this effort is Nir Golan, an Israeli lawyer and legal tech thought leader. I asked him for his thoughts on the human connection to technology and he responded by saying:

> *"I think that legal technology is a great thing, so long as it solves real needs that we have, and isn't just cool to have, as is the case with a lot of the tech we see today. I'm a tech lawyer. I've been representing tech companies and start-ups for the past 14 years, so I'm very excited about technology and an avid user of technology. But technology needs to be part of a well-designed solution that meets users' needs and is easy and intuitive to use. It has to work well as part of our daily lives, with a big emphasis on user experience. Otherwise, people won't use it. At work, we use technology that works well with our problems and processes. We spend a lot of time thinking about and redesigning processes so that the people, process, and technology will work in sync.*
>
> *"One thing I feel very strongly about is integrating the tech element only after the people and process part is clear. I've spent the past few months doing that—understanding our problems, needs, and processes. The questions that our team (which includes our IT team) asks are, 'What is the problem we are trying to solve? Do we need technology to solve it?' And if technology is needed to help and save us time, we will definitely use it. We are a very tech-oriented company. The IT team and I were meeting with a tech vendor the other day (for our legal processes) and the questions we asked the vendor*

> were, 'Why do we need this? What does your product do that our existing suite of products/tech does not do?'"

Raj Goyle, a legal tech founder, adds:

> "Don't be intimidated by legal tech—embrace it! Legal tech solutions aren't here to take jobs away from corporate legal departments or fire your law firms—they're here to ensure you can effectively mitigate risk and navigate your matters while operating as efficiently and economically as possible."

Legal technology is not here to strike fear into your heart or to intimidate you. It's not here to replace you. It is here to *help you* and *help you help those you want to help*. What it is here to do is to automate the routine, the standardized, and the time-consuming. It is here to allow you to spend your time more productively, to bring more value to your role and to those you work with and work for.

If your job consists solely of tasks that are low risk and can be automated, then yes, legal tech will replace you. If your job is a mix of low-value and low-risk work and other higher-risk and more strategic work, then legal tech is here to take some work away from you. At this stage of legal tech's evolution, legal tech can replace tasks and some jobs, but it is not here to replace all that you represent and do.

As Raj Goyle noted, the most important part of understanding legal tech is its role. Its role is as a facilitator, an enabler, and a toolset. It's the people and the processes that make all the difference. Technology should fit naturally into the people and process equation.

Chapter 4

The Legal Technology–Legal Innovation Connection

"Consumers of legal services are demanding lower costs, better outcomes, and more transparency from the legal profession."

THE TERMS "LEGAL TECHNOLOGY" AND "LEGAL INNOVATION" are frequently bandied about, especially on social media. Because of their wide use, defining the terms is a challenging task—and often an exercise in defining what they are not. In the next few chapters, you will read about people engaged in not just understanding and defining what these terms mean, but in creating legal technology, legal innovations, or both.

TECHNOLOGY AND INNOVATION

Legal technology and legal innovation are different things. Innovation can take place without technology, and it can happen on all scales, from the individual to industry wide. Jordan Galvin, who came to law after studying chemistry and physics, discovered this after taking a different approach to presenting information and finding this approach to be a marked advantage:

> *"I remember in my 1L Contracts class, the professor said we could bring one page, front and back, to the exam. We could do whatever we wanted to the paper and use whatever notes or images we thought useful. So, I condensed all of my notes into a comprehensive flowchart of 1L contracts law and fit it onto the allowed sheet. When I got to the exam and looked around, all my classmates had papers with zero margins and eight-point font, seemingly trying to cram an entire semester's worth of notes onto one sheet. My first thought was, 'Are you kidding? There is absolutely no utility in that document.' Throughout the rest of law school, whenever there was an open-book exam, my classmates would bring their 40-page outlines, and I would show up with my 5-page flowchart. Then I met Dan Linna, a leading expert on legal innovation, and realized that there was both a need and opportunity for this type of thinking in the legal industry, and that I could actually make a career out of this.*

> *"Looking forward, though, I am careful how I frame what my passions are. Perhaps I am interested in 'legal technology and innovation,' but I'm not sure that explains much. I'm passionate about improving the way legal organizations do business. I'm passionate about rethinking how legal services are delivered. I'm passionate about working with practicing attorneys, not just to make them better at what they do, but to make them happier with what they do. If*

technology and other initiatives fit measurable business objectives, I'm all for it."

Consider process improvement, which is essentially a refining of existing business processes. There are several ways to do this, including the well-known methods called Lean and Six Sigma. Using these methods can do wonders to improve existing processes or allow the adoption of new and better ones.

Or consider the role of technology in facilitating financial transactions. Technology has led to the creation of new types of transactions and companies such as Kabbage, a company that provides funding to small businesses through an automated lending platform using data analytics.

Another example is the creation of blockchain and the rise of cryptocurrencies. In the legal space, technology has both made new ways of delivering legal services possible and made standard, routine, and time-consuming legal tasks easier and quicker to accomplish. But those new ways first had to be thought of, and that's where innovation comes in.

Carlos Gamez, vice president of product and growth at the legal tech company, Termscout, makes the point that legal processes and legal technologies must be designed with enforceability in mind:

> *"For instance, an online dispute resolution system needs to ensure constitutional, legal, and regulatory protections to safeguard against challenges on the arbitral award's execution, computable contracts need to form valid contracts per contract law to be enforceable, and so on.*
>
> *"Often, an innovation is not usable in the legal space until it is recognized as legally admissible or permissible. For instance, machine-learning technology applied to predictive coding existed for many years before courts allowed it to be used in e-discovery. Some innovations, like do-it-yourself legal document creation, have pushed*

the boundaries of what constitutes unauthorized practice of law, changing the way individuals self-solve for legal needs."

MARKET DEMANDS AND INNOVATION

Consumers of legal services are demanding lower costs, better outcomes, and more transparency from the legal profession. They are also demanding more holistic, business-minded solutions to their problems. This requires some adaptation on the part of attorneys who have, generally, been taught to think in a certain way, write in a certain way, and behave in a certain way—a way that may or may not make it easier to learn new skills, acquire new knowledge, and put both to use right away.

Perhaps it depends on one's viewpoint. Dennis Kennedy, who is well-known for his work in promoting innovation and the use of technology in practicing law, notes:

"I love the definition of innovation used by Alan Weiss, who is one of the foremost thinkers on consulting and on innovation: 'Innovation is applied (pragmatic) creativity.' For me, innovation focuses a lot on business models. Some describe innovation as happening in the realm of 'why' and 'what' and technology is more solidly in the realm of 'how.' Legal technology is about tools."

Gerald Glover III, a lawyer and legal technologist, defines legal innovation as

"new ways to complete legal work that provide more value to clients. To me, innovation means thinking 'outside the box' and doing things better than they have been done in the past. In practice, it means bringing a more diverse set of professional colleagues and more diverse skill sets to the table to solve legal challenges and create more comprehensive business solutions. This represents a new approach to the traditional methods used by large law firms. Here at

Davis Wright Tremaine, we generally think of innovation in regard to each specific client. We try to bring a fresh perspective to each project, so that we can create a solution that puts our client in a better strategic position than they were before. That enables true progress in business operations and is not simply a different way of accomplishing the same goal."

Jason Barnwell, general manager for digital transformation of corporate, external, and legal at Microsoft, incorporates customers' needs into his "shorthand" definition of meaningful innovation, which is,

"serving a job to be done in a new way that delivers meaningful value for my customers. This definition invokes several assumptions.

"First, innovation often benefits from technology but does not require technology. Many impactful innovations are built on critically examining how we do something with a recaptured naiveté. The story about the doctor who first championed hand washing is an example of someone who applied a beginner's mind and experimentation to examine a problem with a fresh perspective. He instituted a simple process that would eventually save countless lives.

"Second, innovation should aim to deliver meaningful value for stakeholders, and thereby achieve escape velocity. Technologists often look past this principle out of sheer excitement for the possibility of the new or the so-called revolutionary. We love trying out new things—but a measured experimentation is necessary because it pushes us to test hypotheses. It also lets us explore approaches that may jump the divide between improvement and innovation. We must focus on driving change that will eventually yield business impact. It is tempting to apply digital transformation to our most

complicated scenarios, even when they don't happen often. Modest innovation applied to a process that happens on a large scale can be more valuable than grand innovation applied to an infrequent process that is well- served by experts.

"Third, I think of innovation as needing to serve a job to be done. I cannot overstate how important it is to understand what customers are trying to accomplish—what causes them to welcome assistance. This can be a challenge because achieving an impactful, innovative solution may require going beyond what they will tell you if you ask.

"Even the most sophisticated customers may not yet have fully examined this. Many simply know that what they currently have is broken and that there must be a better way. To overcome this challenge, try to see what your customers want to accomplish, end-to-end, with a deep respect for the qualitative aspects of your experience that may influence their selection behavior."

Legal technology is inherently innovative because legal technology seeks to develop tools to improve how things have been done before. This makes sense, considering that what has often happened is automation of a manual process or manual task, or making a manual task less onerous by the deployment of a piece of technology. One can be innovative within the legal industry without needing to have created or deployed a legal technology tool.

Some companies have innovated to maintain competitive advantage; think of Apple and the iPhone. Companies may also innovate in an effort to be proactive toward potential new problems coming down the pike (*e.g.,* new privacy restrictions on the use of data) or to enable more robust business growth through more efficient and flexible processes and procedures (*e.g.,* moving from a paper-based office to a digital one). Within the legal industry, says Kunoor Chopra, who founded LawScribe:

"Innovation is something legal departments are doing every day to improve how they work. We have seen a lot of innovation in contracts technologies recently, including products incorporating elements of artificial intelligence. These can predict what the outcome will be of a new contract negotiation based on previously executed contracts and past results, allowing people to make better negotiation decisions before entering into long-term agreements. Innovation in contracts generally is a place to watch."

Marlene Gebauer, co-host of a popular legal podcast, *Geek in Review*, and assistant director of innovation at the law firm of Mayer Brown, has this to say about innovation:

"In law, technology has allowed us access to a wealth of data we never had before. We must make use of it—the analytics, the combined organization knowledge—or we risk being the buggy-whip manufacturer in a world full of cars. We push analytics out in a variety of ways and for a variety of purposes. Some examples are evaluations of judges and opposition, looking for filing trends that impact ultimate decisions, predictions of the best experts for a matter, and deal points, clauses, and related trends. We do the same with organizational knowledge, including client knowledge. We have been able to apply technology to experience sets to determine the best possible decision and to bubble up records for review.

"Technology has also afforded us the means to automate. End-to-end contract management is growing in importance and we have been able to automate drafting and review. We have also improved our best-practice document search by using machine-learning tools that understand context. We hope to use this technology on other internal document sets."

Automated end-to-end contract management? That is systemic change, all right. But when it comes to legal innovation, foremost to keep in mind is that there is more than one way to innovate, and what might seem like modest innovations can make a real difference—to a team, to a company, to the delivery of legal services where they are needed most.

GETTING INTO LEGAL TECHNOLOGY

There are many roads to involvement in legal technology. Cat Moon followed the well-known approach of jumping in at the deep end:

"In 2006, I opened a boutique law firm with two other women … [and] became the self-appointed tech expert for the firm. I simply had to figure it all out … I learned about human-centered design and have come to realize that the design process and mindset are critical to the process of building useful technology. We've got to figure out the human problems to be solved before we build the solutions. (Design is also critical to delivering legal services, by the way.) … People don't focus on the problems enough."

There is something else Moon would like lawyers to understand about legal technology:

"It's really hard to build a really, really good technology that solves real problems. If lawyers want good technology, they must be willing to invest the time and energy to collaborate with those who can build the technology, to do the hard work that leads to the right solutions.

"And likewise, those who are building legal tech must be willing to engage deeply in the human-centered design process to discover the real problems, before they start building solutions."

Another story of innovation comes from Nehal Madhani. Nehal was a practicing attorney at a well-known international law firm when he felt inspired to try to make his own legal practice more efficient. He taught himself programming and founded Alt Legal, a company that offers cloud-based trademark docketing software. Nehal says of his experience:

> "My path to creating Alt Legal wasn't direct. It was during law school when I realized that my passion was creating and growing businesses. I launched my first business (an online classifieds service for students) during college; unfortunately, it failed during my second year of law school.

> "After law school, I was eager to gain practical legal knowledge, so I joined the restructuring group at Kirkland & Ellis. At the start of my fourth year at Kirkland, I felt restless. I saw so many inefficiencies across the legal industry—so many hours spent doing tasks that should be easy and safe to automate.

> "In 2013, I left the firm and learned computer programming to launch my first legal tech venture, a marketplace connecting a network of vetted lawyers with businesses needing legal advice. While starting this venture and securing its intellectual property (IP), I experienced the inefficiencies of trademark prosecution firsthand. Most of the steps were manual, and tracking filings and deadlines felt archaic. I spoke with other IP professionals who echoed the frustrations I felt; and in 2014, I shut down the marketplace and launched Alt Legal to automate the way trademark professionals create, manage, and analyze their trademarks."

Innovation happens for many reasons—necessity, desire for change, or just a willingness to experiment. Technological advances have opened the door for new ways of performing tasks and new ways of creating things. Technology has led to plenty of innovations, such as easier ways to apply for trademarks, analyze contracts, use data to formulate a litigation strategy, or simply create a set of documents.

These new ways of doing things resulted from individuals wanting to do things differently. Wanting to do things differently, however, can be achieved with or without technology. One can improve a problematic process through process improvement techniques or speed up a sales cycle by creating and providing easy access to a new standard contract template. Innovation can happen with or without technology, but technology certainly has opened the door to innovations that could not have happened without it.

Chapter 5

Technology and Its Seductive Nature

"The seductive quality of technology—slick, shiny, groundbreaking—has too often led to doing just the opposite, resulting in a solution in search of a problem."

THE LEGAL INDUSTRY HAS LONG ADHERED TO TRADITION, and tension arises when tradition meets a new reality. The reality is that even the legal world is not a static place. It is evolving and incredibly dynamic. Legal technology seeks to acknowledge this and align the services of legal service providers with those seeking legal services. It has two aspects.

One is the creation of technologies that enable better legal services and better delivery of legal services; and the other is a movement of people and ideas aimed at making the staid legal industry into one that is enabled by technology, one that is inclusive rather than exclusive, and one that is client centered.

TECHNO-OPTIMISM

There are several pitfalls along the way. Quinten Steenhuis, senior housing attorney and network administrator for Greater Boston Legal Services, can speak to one of the biggest pitfalls and his approach to avoiding it:

"I think it's easy to fall into the trap of techno-optimism. Before reaching for technology, you need to have a good understanding of the process that you want to improve. Sometimes technology just speeds up a bad process, leading to efficient injustice. That said, the ubiquity of mobile phones and high-speed Internet access make technology a much better solution than it was, even 10 years ago.

"Document assembly is the technology we use the most. I'm a big evangelist of an open-source tool called Docassemble, created by Jonathan Pyle at Philadelphia Legal Assistance. Our legal aid clients are poor and burdened by an endless amount of paperwork and forms and appointments to keep, just to maintain the thin web of support they have in place. The $2 for the T [subway] is a barrier. Paying for childcare or taking a day off work can threaten their ability to make it through the month. The more we can use technology to help reduce the need for them to come into our office, the better. Docassemble is one way we make things easier for our clients. We use Docassemble together with our case management system to send clients retainers and releases that they can sign right on their phones.

"Several years ago, I created a project called Massachusetts Defense for Eviction (MADE), which has allowed us to completely transform

our help for tenants facing eviction. We have always offered a once-a-week eviction clinic, but not everybody could attend. MADE is what I call a clinic in a box. It walks tenants through the forms they need to defend themselves in court, in six different languages, written at a sixth-grade reading level. It has help text and videos to explain the law along the way. It reminds tenants about their court dates with text messages automatically. We're up to about 200 people a month using it now, in our clinics, at the Court Service Center, and completely on their own at home. I'd love to see more projects like MADE that can serve different legal needs."

DEFINING ARTIFICIAL INTELLIGENCE

The "trap of techno-optimism" is real—and few things attract both techno-optimism and misunderstanding as much as robots and AI. They are both often thought of, or presented, as slick and shiny and groundbreaking. You've likely seen a YouTube clip or two of a robot jumping or stacking boxes or even interacting in a human-like way with a person. Robots are now part of health care, manufacturing, and space exploration—all fields where innovation is usually prized. Well, guess what? Although the legal field is coming to prize innovation, legal technology is not about replacing attorneys with robots—I. Robot, Esq., will never appear in a courtroom. Legal technology is not about robots at all. As for AI, it is true that many legal technology tools use elements of AI.

So, just what is AI? For this, I turned to someone who literally wrote a book on the topic,[3] Joshua Walker, a leading expert on AI in law, who had this to say on the topic:

"Artificial intelligence has become a marketing meme. At its core, the term relates to models, which give rise to algorithms that are addressed to aspects of thinking, perception, and action. (Thanks to

---

[3] Joshua Walker. *On Legal AI*. Full Court Press, 2019.

the late Professor Patrick Winston of MIT for this paraphrased definition.) I think people are massively overusing this term. However, the hype ratio for AI is not as high as it was for Bitcoin at its height. The reality is that AI is addressing myriad projects successfully, but that reality is much murkier and much harder to realize than people think. It has so much to do with the data. I say in the book that 'data is the mother of AI and math is the father.' It is about applied mathematics operating on data sets—and most raw data sets are a total entropic mess. So, before you do any functional algorithm– or model-building, you must clean the data. And if you want to turn that AI potential into law, you must realize that we are talking applied math working across historical events that are essentially legal, highly complex qualitative events. That definition, in my view, is probably the number one thing to keep in mind.

"But, in general, AI is a marketing meme; you should ignore it and really think instead about the data and the mathematics. If you can do that, suddenly it becomes traceable. The other thing that happens, when you define AI applications as data and mathematical models on top of those data, is that the data really matter in terms of the ultimate identity of the finished product. Every legal AI 'thing' is like a fingerprint. They're not the same at all even when they perform the same function, and even when they perform the same function with similar results."

A final note about AI as it relates to the legal industry is the lack of an ethical or regulatory framework surrounding its use. This is an important consideration. All technologies, including those incorporating AI elements, are developed by human beings who are imperfect, who carry and apply their own biases—biases of which they may or may not be aware.

Consider that an algorithm may not be fair because of an area's demographics. "Average statistics can mask discrimination among regions or subpopulations and avoiding it may require customizing algorithms for each subset. That explains why any regulations aimed at decreasing local or small-group biases are likely to reduce the potential for scale advantages from AI, which is often the motivation for using it in the first place."[4]

There have been efforts to establish a regulatory framework for artificial intelligence, such as the Algorithmic Accountability Act of 2019 and a revised version of the legislation, the Algorithmic Accountability Act of 2022.[5] Both proposed acts would require "mandatory self-assessment of their AI systems, including disclosure of firm usage of AI systems, their development process, system design, and training, as well as the data gathered and used."[6]

The duty of technology competence points in one clear direction as it relates to AI and other technologies: Lawyers should consider using a technology if it can be beneficial to those they mean to help, but the ethics of using technology must also be considered. "Technological advancements should make the judicial system better, not worse. So, in the words of one federal district court judge, 'don't freak out.'"[7]

LOOK TO THE PROCESS: A OR B?

Imagine two companies. Someone in Company B reads an article written by someone in Company A that claims legal technology has helped Company A save millions of dollars and made its employees happier, more productive, and more efficient, leading to Company A's significantly increased bottom line. Upon reading this article, and after further research by the executive team, Company B decides to

---

[4] François Candelon, Rodolphe Charme di Carlo, Midas De Bondt, and Theodoros Evgeniou, "AI Regulation Is Coming," *Harvard Business Review* (September–October 2021).
[5] H.R. 6580. Algorithmic Accountability Act of 2022. 117th Congress (2021–2022).
[6] *Id.*
[7] Kip Nelson, "Legal Ethics 2.0: How Emerging Technologies Are Creating Novel Ethical Dilemmas," *Appellate Issues*, Winter 2022. American Bar Association.

invest money into that same technological solution. Company B expects the same results as Company A.

However, a year later, Company B was unable to replicate the success of its competitor and is now left with an expensive, underused tool that is understood by only a few employees and despised by many others. Company B was an unwitting party seduced by a shiny piece of technology that suited its successful competitor but not Company B. Company B may never have looked at the differences between how Company A works and how Company B works, and thus adopted the technology without a real suitability assessment.

One way to avoid spending money on technology for technology's sake is to take the time to understand the problem you are trying to solve before building a product that is supposed to solve it. Michael L. Bloom, who has (in his words) "been curating spaces for students and professionals to make mistakes—and learn from them—since 2009," is an advocate of this approach. He founded Praktio, a provider of interactive online learning games and exercises for developing practical contracts skills and know-how. At the University of Michigan Law School, Bloom was the founding director of the Transactional Lab & Clinic. He says:

> *"Useful tech development and adoption starts with understanding the problem you're trying to solve and building a solution that solves it, ideally involving the various stakeholders, users, and decision makers throughout, to keep you aligned on the right goals and to get the buy-in needed for the technology to be used effectively.*

> *"A great way to avoid building or using technology for technology's sake is to start small and cheap, which often means exploring the least tech-heavy solutions first (which might be no tech)! One way to do that is to map out a process that will let you see opportunities for improvement, and then to map those improvements onto a simple grid, with one axis labeled 'high impact—low impact' and the other labeled 'high cost—low cost' [Figure 3]. Then you can make*

your list of things to try, giving first priority to items that have high impact but are low cost."

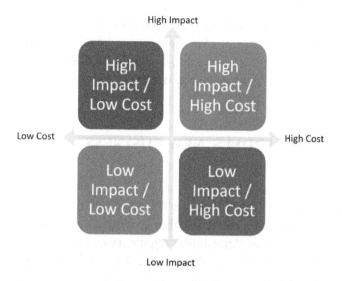

Figure 3. Cost and Impact Matrix. *Courtesy of Michael L. Bloom.*

To succeed as a lawyer in today's world requires a far broader skill set than knowing the law. The skills now being demanded of lawyers include collaboration, project management, quantitative literacy, and understanding data analytics. The ability to resist the over-optimistic idea that purchasing technology and turning it on will solve all one's problems is also among these newly required skills. The problem that is to be solved must first be understood—that is, the factors that created the problem and the experience of those dealing with it directly must be understood by any would-be problem solvers. The seductive quality of technology—slick, shiny, ground-breaking—has too often led to doing just the opposite, resulting in a solution in search of a problem.

It is commonly held that putting a technological solution in place will resolve all the existing problems within a law firm or a legal department. But problems within a law practice can arise from any number of areas—people not following a given process, a process not functioning as envisioned (or some combination of the two), not having enough processes in place to handle a given workload, and so on. Without a handle on what problems exist or why they exist, how can one reasonably expect to deploy a piece of technology to fix them?

As Mark A. Cohen noted in *Forbes*, "To be meaningful, technology must be relevant to a material client use-case."[8] Moreover, simple enthusiasm for technology also overlooks one of technology's greatest contributions to the legal industry: the creation of new business models.

NEW MODELS, NEW BUSINESS

Technology has led to the disaggregation of legal work. The practice of law and the delivery of legal services are becoming separate things. Buyers of legal services are turning to alternative legal service providers and niche firms. Alternative legal services providers provide many of the services of a traditional law firm. These services include things such as litigation support, legal research, document review, e-discovery, and compliance. Individuals engaged in delivering legal services are now using process improvement and data analytics to lower the cost of legal services and deliver better outcomes.

LegalZoom is a prime example of a company offering legal services via a new, direct-to-consumer and lawyer-free business model. LegalZoom became successful not just because of technology, but also because of a tireless focus on the client (consumer). This client-centered approach has either long evaded the grasp of lawyers or has been outright ignored by them.

Companies that adopt new business models can also demonstrate the power of employing legal professionals who can draw upon a broad array of skills. These firms have well-tested processes in place and, most important, they have an unwavering focus on the needs of the consumer of legal services. In both the present and the future, the successful lawyers and successful law practices will be those that are

---

[8] Mark A. Cohen, "New Business Models, Not Technology, Will Transform the Legal Industry," *Forbes*, November 8, 2018.

focused on consumers. Technology can help (and is helping) to facilitate this.

Traditional models of performing legal services have not been aligned with what legal consumers have wanted. These models persisted because consumers had few, if any, alternatives. Some may also have trusted their attorneys to have their clients' best interests at heart. Technology is bringing transparency by opening the curtains and shining a light on how law is practiced.[9]

Still, lawyers and the legal profession remain highly resistant to change. Technology will not fix that. Overcoming this resistance will require several things. First, legal technology advocates must meet lawyers and other professional individuals where they are by understanding their needs and their concerns.

Second, advocates must educate those professionals to inform them and alleviate their concerns or misunderstanding about technology—as this book is trying to do!

Third, practitioners should embrace, encourage, and incentivize collaboration among lawyers, legal professionals, technologists, and others.

Fourth, patience will be needed, although change is happening even as these words are written.

Pressure from consumers will aid this progress as they become better educated about what options, in addition to the traditional ones, are available to help with their legal needs. As this happens, legal consumers will be attracted to those providers who can best deliver better outcomes and services at lower costs. It cannot be overstated that the real impact of legal technology will come from the new ways of practicing law that were developed because of introducing technology into the mix.

---

[9] Mark A. Cohen noted, in his article on legal business models (note 8), that "Legal technology is a good news/bad news story. The good news is that technology's utility as a tool to help solve law's wicked problems—notably the democratization of access to and improvement of the delivery of legal services—is now widely recognized, if not applied."

SOCIALIZING LEGAL TECH

Social media has become a popular and influential means of communicating about legal technology.

I started my blog because I wanted to share the stories I had been told in my many conversations with legal tech leaders. I knew that if I truly wanted to learn about the legal technology space, I needed to listen to those at the front lines trying to facilitate change and create new tools and solutions.

I then started to expand my presence online to social media. My social media approach was simple: a deliberate effort to share the lessons I was learning through my interviews with leading legal figures. I love to listen to the experiences of others and believe that others can benefit from the stories that I am told.

There was another factor driving my use of social media. I graduated from law school at a time when legal jobs were scarce. I didn't want to work for a law firm, which only made the job search more difficult because in-house roles typically require experience.

The only way for me to find work was to build relationships with others—to network. I didn't realize it at the time, but the networking efforts I made helped me see and understand the power of relationships. My use of social media has helped me develop networking and relationship-building skills that have led to countless new opportunities, including those within legal technology.

I never would have the role I now have were it not for my sustained social media efforts. I was able to read, respond, and connect with leading legal tech creators and founders; and it was those connections that truly lit my passion for legal technology.

One leader in the use of social media within the legal space is Alex Su. Although he started posting about legal technology, he is now well-known for his humorous memes making fun of lawyers and lawyers' behavior. A few years ago, I sat down with Alex to talk about his social media journey. One of the questions I asked him was what had surprised him most when he began posting on social media, and what he would say to other lawyers who were thinking about creating content using social media. He responded:

> "I've been surprised at how many lawyers read my content. When I went to a conference in New York, I met many people who already knew me from LinkedIn. In fact, some of them, including law firm partners, privately told me that while they really enjoyed reading my content, they wouldn't be caught dead liking or commenting on my posts! That took me by surprise—both the seniority of the lawyers reading my content, and the number of people who read and never engage. That's part of the reason why I keep posting, because even if I don't get a lot of likes or comments, I know I'm getting through to my audience.

> "If you are thinking of posting on social media, I'd say you should have a clearly defined goal. It can be easy to fall into the trap of chasing likes and comments for their own sake. More attention isn't always better. My goal has been to help promote my employer's legal tech offering and to gain visibility among industry experts. I have a lot more freedom than, say, a lawyer at a law firm, to post controversial content, which is exactly why I do it. It's one of my assets. But that doesn't mean there aren't other paths to success. ... If you look at some of the other leading law firm lawyers on social media, you'll find that each person has their own voice that is aligned with their day job.

> "Social media is a very interesting space, and the rules are constantly changing. To do well, you've got to try new things, experiment, and iterate. It's not for everyone, and it can feel risky. But it can also help you find opportunities you never could have imagined. That's certainly been my experience."

Another social media leader in law is David Lat. He is a former lawyer and the founder of the legal commentary and news website called *Above the Law* (ATL). He now publishes a well-followed digital newsletter, "Original Jurisdiction." His career has taken several twists and turns. I asked him about the choices he had made. He explained:

> *"I went straight through from college to law school without any grand plan. I didn't have a sense of what it was like to be a lawyer; going to law school just seemed like a natural thing to do for someone like me with an interest in writing and speaking. My first few years after law school were conventional. I clerked for the Ninth Circuit, for the (wonderful) Judge Diarmuid F. O'Scannlain in Portland, and then returned to the New York area to work as a litigation associate at the law firm of Wachtell Lipton. After a few years, I moved over to the U.S. Attorney's Office for New Jersey. I had interned in that office during my 1L summer and loved it, and I had always thought I might go back.*

> *"While I was at the U.S. Attorney's Office, my career took an unusual turn. I had always loved writing, going back to my days as a columnist for the* **Harvard Crimson** *and my time as editor in chief of my high school's opinion journal, and although I did a lot of legal writing as an assistant U.S. attorney, I wasn't really doing any writing that didn't involve Bluebooking. I was looking for a way to do some nonlegal writing.*

> *"It was 2004, and this thing called 'blogging' was on the rise. So I started a blog called 'Underneath Their Robes,' which offered 'news, gossip, and colorful commentary about the federal judiciary,' which is a subject of long-standing interest to me.*

"The blog did well. In November 2005, in an interview with the **New Yorker,** *I revealed myself as the author of 'Underneath Their Robes.' A few weeks later, I left the U.S. Attorney's Office to blog full time."*

I also asked him about ATL. I wanted to understand how he came to start it and how it has evolved. He told me:

"The impetus behind **Above the Law** *was like the impetus behind 'Underneath Their Robes': to bring greater transparency to an often opaque, occasionally confusing world—the judiciary for 'Underneath Their Robes,' and the legal profession writ large for* **ATL.** *I also wanted to offer some humor and entertainment, two things that are sorely needed in the legal profession.*

*"**ATL** started with a lot of gossip and humor, but as time went on, we found there was a real hunger for certain kinds of news and analysis in the legal profession that weren't being provided by existing outlets—for example, detailed information about salaries and bonuses at law firms, or an alternative to the* **U.S. News & World Report** *rankings for law schools. So we started to fill that gap in the market. It was still about increasing transparency, but also had the more specific mission of helping people make better decisions—e.g., which law school should I attend, or which law firm should I work for. In recent years,* **ATL** *has been a strong voice for increasing diversity in the legal profession, and I'm proud of* **ATL's** *work on that issue—which started well before the current focus on diversity and inclusion."*

In an age driven by technological advancement, social media has become an influential and powerful tool for informing, inspiring, and building relationships. It facilitates the creation of communities, such as the ones that Alex and David have built for themselves. Social media also can be used for more nefarious purposes, such as the spreading of misinformation or misleading information, as has been made all too clear in the political sphere. However, the value of social media very much lies in what you make of it. For me, whether it be for learning about something, like legal technology, connecting with others, or just sharing my own thoughts and opinions, social media remains a vital and incredibly effective means of building a community, a brand, or even the foundations of a successful company.

Chapter 6

Innovation in Action

"News flash: That WordPress website and so-called AI tool to capture more billable hours are not innovative, and they certainly do not qualify as the sort of meaningful business transformation that clients are looking for."—Daniel Farris

I'S TIME TO SEE WHAT INNOVATION LOOKS LIKE IN ACTION. I'll start.

I was once a member of a small legal team for a prominent international manufacturing company. The business was growing fast, as was the legal team's workload, particularly in the number of contracts to review and negotiate. We needed a system to manage contract intake, review, and storage. First, we worked on establishing what such a system would have to accomplish, including what essential features and workflows would look like, and then we went about creating the system using an existing tool as the basis for it. The intent was to establish a much clearer, more consistent, and partially automated contract workflow.

Although the work was not finished when I left the company, the effects of the work that had already been done were being felt, which encouraged the team to continue despite numerous setbacks. A company with a very heavy workload and a limited budget will often attempt to build a new tool or process internally. This was my first taste of innovation—the good, the bad, and the ugly.

Daniel Farris is someone who understands firsthand the struggle to get others to learn, to create, and to change. He is a former software engineer, a founder of the legal technology firm, Proxy, and a technology and intellectual property attorney. I asked him about his experience building technology and where things stand with respect to the relationship between creating technology and the adoption of technology by the legal industry. He had this to say:

> *"For starters, most start-ups fail, regardless of industry. In law, however, there seems to be an inordinate number of companies that have not yet identified the demographic and market changes driving the industry. For example, did you know that approximately 75 percent to 80 percent of corporate legal work was done by lawyers at law firms before 2008? Since then, only 20 percent to 25 percent is done by 'outside' lawyers, according to some reports. The majority of the work is handled in-house, or by alternative legal services providers. That's a useful bit of information when considering the prospective buyers of your legal tech product, and yet most solutions on the market still primarily cater to firm lawyers.*

> *"And some products try to do too much, purporting to be the only application a lawyer will need in her day to accomplish everything on her plate. Even if true, which those claims never are, people do not actually work like that. We tend to use a lot of applications for specific purposes. Other products are too narrow, appealing to only*

a small niche of users. And still more claim to automate everything or to use AI to complete tasks for lawyers—only, lawyers don't want someone or something else making decisions for them."

Much of the rest of this chapter features a description, in Farris's words, of his experience and the lessons learned through wearing the many hats that he did. Below, as Farris makes clear, true innovation is often messy, uncertain, and involves a series of steps forward and steps back.[10]

HOW TO DO IT RIGHT

Step 1: Don't Be a Law Firm

With apologies to any law firm attorneys or chief innovation officers who may be reading this: If you want to build good legal tech products and services, don't be a law firm—at least not a large one. Perhaps the only trend more prominent than the influx of money to legal technology is the propensity of AmLaw 200[11] firms to engage in "innovation theater." News flash: That WordPress website and so-called AI tool to capture more billable hours are not innovative, and they certainly do not qualify as the sort of meaningful business transformation that clients are looking for.

Real innovation involves risk-taking, failure, creative thinking, and flexibility—behaviors and traits that large law firms generally abhor, regardless of what they may say about it. Real innovation requires design thinking to align technology with meaningful process improvement. Law firms haven't changed their delivery or services models meaningfully in decades, so it is foolish to believe that they possess the ability to challenge the status quo when it comes to technological adoption, user experience, or feature sets.

---

[10] This chapter is contributed by Daniel Farris and is used with permission.
[11] The AmLaw200 is *The American Lawyer*'s list of U.S. law firms ranked 101–200 by gross revenue.

Instead, firms are likely to continue to engage in innovation theater, either intentionally or because they do not understand the difference between apparent change and actual change. When law firms hire chief innovation officers but fail to fund or empower them meaningfully, form innovation or ideas committees, engage in hackathons, or tout the adoption of new technologies for the use of their internal attorneys or tracking hourly billing, please do not confuse this with innovation. It is not. This is theater—activities intended to give the appearance of change without bringing about actual change.

Perhaps the single greatest barrier to real innovation for law firms is the traditional financial model of such firms. Innovation takes investment and the expectation of near-term losses for long-term gain. Law firms generally manage their finances with a short-term focus, with annual performance (and sometimes monthly or even daily performance) the primary concern. This is fundamentally at odds with what is needed for the creation, testing, implementation, and adoption of new technology.

Step 2: Know Your Audience

Developing good software, whether legal or otherwise, starts with people and processes. Technology adoption, like most other consumer behavior, is as much about connecting with the buyer emotionally as it is about any specific feature set or promised outcome. This means understanding what your target audience really wants and needs, even when they cannot articulate it themselves.

By way of example, 10 years ago few people were clamoring for new ways to communicate in 280-character snippets, but Twitter has been successful. You would have been hard pressed to find anyone who was asking to get in cars with strangers, but Uber and Lyft understood that the market was ripe for a new type of service model. The most successful technology often understands users and anticipates consumers' real desires even before the consumers know they want or need the product.

In other words, empathy is a key component in product development. Understanding not only what your target audience wants but why they want it is key.

By way of example, when NMBL Technologies started to develop Proxy—a legal workflow management tool—they interviewed as many in-house lawyers as possible. The lawyers were asking for a wide array of features—task management, document management, reporting, delegation, document automation, collaboration tools, and more. NMBL listened but asked questions to understand why users were asking for these features. It turns out that many in-house counsel feel overwhelmed, out of control, buried by administrative tasks, as if they serve too many masters. Thus, in framing Proxy, NMBL sought to do more than build a product with features that users said they wanted. In fact, NMBL expressly rejected some of the direction from users because the features didn't help in solving the problem, which was that in-house counsel wanted to feel more in control of their workloads. In other words, the solution wasn't better workflow management—it was giving users back a sense of agency and control. To do this effectively, NMBL had to connect with Proxy users emotionally, not just intellectually.

That said, basic market dynamics continue to apply. Before the recession that began in 2008, most of the corporate legal work was done by lawyers at law firms. Today, corporate legal departments and the in-house lawyers who staff them handle the majority of all corporate legal matters. Today, too, the cost of legal representation continues to price out more and more of the general public, making access to justice more difficult than ever. And yet, most legal technology products and services on the market are still geared toward, or outright designed for, lawyers at Big Law firms. This has created large market segments that are unserved or underserved, creating opportunities for aspiring legal technology developers.

Understanding who the users are, what motivates them, what issues they have, and what they really need is critical for building good legal technology. Products with the best features imaginable will fail if they do not engage users. The focus should be on solving problems for the audience of technology users, even if those problems are not or cannot be clearly articulated by the users themselves.

Step 3: Accept That Process Is Everything

Once an innovator knows what the prospective users truly want, the next step is to understand how to deliver it. In this regard, process is everything. Many things in the practice of law are archaic and arbitrary, relying on tradition at all costs. This is why design thinking is so desperately needed in the legal industry. Automating bad processes only amplifies trouble and leads to bad (or worse) results.

Design thinking involves an iterative process of seeking first to understand the users, and then challenging assumptions and redefining the problem to identify alternative strategies and solutions that may not be apparent to the users. In other words, design thinking involves deploying empathy in a solutions-based approach, even where the solution involves delivering products or services in a manner not anticipated or requested by the user.

This is perhaps the single best explanation for why some legal technology products succeed where others fail. Those who mistake input from lawyers for system requirements tend to automate bad process. Many developers have been surprised to learn that giving users exactly what they have asked for is not a winning strategy. On the other hand, products that anticipate users' needs and build better processes into their solutions have excelled. Blind adherence to user input is almost never a winning strategy, and dictating process without understanding what users actually want to achieve is equally bad. This is why both design thinking and the development lifecycle (described in greater detail below) are so critical to building good legal technology solutions.

PART DEUX: PROCESS IS STILL EVERYTHING

Process is not only important in what you build, but also in how you build. One of the major challenges for legal technology development is the minimum viable product (MVP) approach, which is common in development but not in the legal industry.

The first step in the MVP process is to define (or redefine) the problem faced by a product's prospective users to obtain a clear understanding of those users' needs. The second step is to challenge assumptions and conceptualize some new solutions. This is followed by building and testing a prototype to capture real and meaningful data on what does work and what does not. Sometimes called the "fail fast" approach, this approach to building technology involves getting beta versions of new software in front of actual users quickly, and then identifying the features and functionality that do not work. Developers then edit or rewrite the software and retest. The premise is that each new iteration is one step closer to the final commercial product.

The challenges to this approach in the legal industry are many. First, failure is not an option for many lawyers. Failure is akin to death ... or worse, malpractice. And yet, any good developer will tell you that failure is an essential part of the process of building good technology. This helps to explain why law firms are bad at technological innovation—they're institutionally and fundamentally opposed to failure.

Second, early-stage failure can be the death knell for commercial success. Lawyers are typically among the latest adopters of technology, which means that they have been conditioned to expect feature sets that have been well-designed and thoroughly tested, with minimal bugs or issues. In contrast, in the MVP approach, the product when first released is intended to have just enough in the way of features to be usable by early adopters, who can then provide feedback for future product development. But if users instead expect complete features and functionality with few to no bugs, they're likely to reject the product outright.

As lawyers are not known for reconsidering prior decisions—especially when it comes to technology—developers can often find themselves in a dilemma. Design thinking is critical for the development of good legal technology products, but asking users to participate in pilot programs and test beta versions of software can turn them off to the product permanently. Perhaps one of the greatest challenges facing legal technology developers is identifying those prospective users who not only understand the problem to be solved but also understand and appreciate the software development process.

Step 4: User Experience Is Everything

The line between consumer and enterprise applications is increasingly blurred. Mobile devices are now, unquestionably, work productivity tools. Developers of legal technology products must treat this understanding as critical, because totally unrelated apps may have greater effects on users' expectations than any competitor's product. Remember, user experience is everything.

Typically, users will expect any technology product to function like the last technology product with which they had a good experience. For legal technology developers, if your user's last two experiences were with a Microsoft Office product (such as Word) on a laptop and Twitter on an iPhone, your competitors—at least when it comes to user experience—are Microsoft, Apple, and Twitter, not Litera or Clio. If you're asking a habitual user of Apple products to move from a Mac to a product that runs only on Windows, you will fail. Fair or not, the user subconsciously expects a Mac.

Good user experience includes ease of use, predictable commands and consistent outcomes, speed, and stability. A good user interface understands not only what a user intends to do, but how and why the user is engaging in the relevant behavior. In this sense, it displays empathy; it is "human."

Perhaps the single most common explanation of the abandonment or underutilization of legal technology products is that the user experience is poor. The complaint that administration and use of the product is less convenient or more time-consuming than completing the underlying task manually is a criticism heard daily.

If you're a developer of legal technology, this problem is real, and it is probably much larger than you think. According to research from PricewaterhouseCoopers,[12] 59 percent of U.S. customers will aban-

---

[12] *See* www.pwc.com/us/en/services/consulting/library/consumer-intelligence-series/future-of-customer-experience.html.

don a company or product that they already enjoy using after only a few bad experiences; 17 percent will walk away after a single bad experience. Imagine the numbers for new customers who don't already know your brand or enjoy using your product. Now imagine the numbers when all your customers are skeptical about or scared of your product to begin with. If the interface isn't approachable, if the system doesn't function as users expect, if the technology doesn't make your users' work lives easier and more efficient, then commercial success is not likely to follow.

Although succeeding in the world of legal technology is a challenge, it can be done. Two illustrative examples are Clio (whose developers used MVP) and Allegory Law.

Clio

A prominent and informative success story is the story of Clio. Clio provides client management software to its 150,000 subscribers with an approval rating from more than 65 bar associations and law societies worldwide. When asked, one of Clio's co-founders, Jack Newton, told the story this way:

> *"I went to the University of Alberta and got a bachelor's degree in computer science. I was excited about the idea of start-ups over the course of getting my computer science degree. One influential book that I read in the early days was Paul Graham's* Hackers and Painters, *which inspired me to think about working at a start-up or even starting my own company. So in my first job out of school, I followed that inspiration and joined a start-up called Chenomx. It was a University of Alberta spin-off company doing some very cool software for medical diagnostics. They used nuclear magnetic resonance to create a very complex spectrum that you could analyze to identify the compounds in a sample of biofluid—blood or cerebral spinal fluid or urine or really any biofluid. You would get an instant readout of all the compounds, all the metabolites in that compound.*

But the numerical optimization problem of trying to deconvolve that spectrum was extremely complex.

"I was software developer number one at this four-person start-up and really kind of fell in love with being in a start-up. We went through the process of raising a million dollars, went through all those early struggles of finding product/market fit, and eventually built out a successful product that was adopted by many of the big pharmaceutical companies. I went back to school to get my master's degree in machine learning because I saw the huge potential that was starting to percolate with machine-learning tools, and I saw the application to what we were doing at Chenomx. I worked my way up to being director of product development. I spent four or five years at Chenomx and eventually got that itch again—I love building start-ups. I loved the work I was doing in life sciences, but I started getting the itch to go out and do my own thing.

"I connected with a lifelong friend, Rian Gauvreau, who had moved to Vancouver and was working on his MBA. We decided to see if there was an idea that energized us—that we thought we might be able to build a company around. I describe me and Rian in those days as being two hammers looking for a nail—two guys looking for an industry that was ripe for transformation.

"And we saw this enormous wave of technological transformation that was cloud computing starting to come down the pike. It was clear to me as a technologist that cloud computing was going to be one of the most transformative waves of technology to come along in a long time—one of those once-in-a-lifetime technology waves where if you catch it, you're going to be able to disrupt incumbents. You're going to be able to drive new adoption in an industry. So we

started looking at industries that we thought might be an especially good fit for cloud computing. At the time, Rian was working as an IT manager at one of Canada's largest law firms. Rian saw how poorly utilized a lot of the firm's internal systems were, saw how much opportunity there was for IT to be better adopted. That was really the inspiration for us, identifying legal as the area we wanted to enter with a product.

"The idea for Clio crystallized during a lunch with a friend of ours who was the director of practice standards at the Law Society of British Columbia. His job was to discipline lawyers when they'd gotten on the wrong side of the ethics rules or had complaints from clients. He told us that most of the conversations he had to have about discipline were with solo and small-firm lawyers—lawyers practicing at the big firms didn't have nearly as many issues as did the small firms and solo practitioners. We pulled at that thread and asked why that was the case.

"He told us that there were several problems. There's the short-handedness that you have in most solos and small firms: if you drop a ball, there's no human infrastructure to catch that for you. You don't have a small army of paralegals and support staff monitoring every key deadline and making sure that stuff gets filed on time and so on. You'd hope to see increased technology adoption by those small firms and solo practitioners, but they don't actually adopt technology all that well either. And when we asked why they didn't adopt technology more, the response was that the small firms and solo practitioners simply don't have the time or the money to invest in complicated on-premises systems. That was the light-bulb moment where we realized that maybe a practice management system that is cloud-based, that is simple and easy to use and deployed over *the cloud, would be a perfect fit for what these solo and small-firm lawyers need.*

"When we did the market research, one of the things that really blew us away was that the vast majority of the legal market is made up of solo practitioners and small firms. About 63 percent of lawyers are in solo practice or small firms and 69 percent of those lawyers practice as solos. It was a real opportunity for us to think about the market in a completely different way and to develop a product that really helped to meet the needs of a vastly underserved segment of the legal population. That was the initial vision for Clio.

"So we got to work and started coding. We were both technology people so we were able to really roll up our sleeves and build Clio ourselves. We built out this tool over the course of a year and launched our beta at the American Bar Association's Techshow in 2008. And the rest is history."

Allegory Law

Allegory Law's story again points to innovation being born out of two things: frustration with a problem and with how things were being done and a willingness to try something new and to experiment to see what works.

Allegory Law offers a cloud-based litigation platform and case management software. Now part of Litera, Allegory Law was founded by Alma Asay, currently senior director of practice innovation and client value at Crowell and Moring, out of her frustration with how things were. She tells the story this way:

"Allegory was inspired by my time as an associate at Gibson Dunn and the frustrations I felt at not having better technology to manage our cases. When I was a first-year associate, the partner for

whom I was working told me, 'I want to see every document in the case. Not just the 'hot' documents—every document.' I knew full well that if I wheeled a cart full of binders into his office, he'd look at me like I was crazy. But I also knew I couldn't say no. I went back to my desk and started typing the relevant portions of every conceivably relevant document, along with details such as date/time/to/from, into an Excel spreadsheet. When I showed him what I was working on (printed and bound, of course, for easy viewing), he told me to keep going.

"Ultimately, we leveraged our support teams to help us create the document digests, which we also shared with in-house counsel, giving everyone on the team an easy grasp on the full scope of evidence. Over the years and across cases, we refined our processes and expanded the scope of what we digested, including incorporating deposition testimony. As I was asked to teach these methods to other litigation teams at the firm, it seemed crazy to me that there wasn't software that could do more of the legwork for us. When I asked our litigation support team about this, they pointed me to CaseMap, which was (unknown to me) already installed on my computer—but when I opened it, I couldn't make heads or tails of it. After doing some additional research, I concluded that the tool we needed didn't exist.

"At the same time, I was nearing the end of my sixth year and thinking about partnership track. I had rushed through school, skipping a few grades, and it occurred to me that, if I ever wanted to try something else, this would be the time. I could always come back and do the required two years in advance of partnership, but if I carried on now and became partner, would I ever leave? Having already achieved more financial security than I had imagined possible grow-

ing up, I decided to make a jump. At first, I planned to do international volunteer work, but a friend had heard me talking about my ideas for litigation software and introduced me to developers in Brooklyn. I met with them and realized that it was possible to bring my ideas to life. Things spiraled from there and Allegory was born."

Another part of Alma's story is in the lessons she learned along the way. There were quite a few:

"I learned so many lessons building Allegory—I think that's the nature of being an entrepreneur, learning anything and everything as quickly as you can. Right away, I learned the biggest lessons: the importance of carefully selecting people and finding the foresight and perspective to see beyond any given difficult moment. These lessons resonate most because of early struggles when I fell out with my original development team and co-founder. The development team had originally agreed to work for equity, but, never having done this before, we didn't have paperwork or good definitions around expectations for how that equity was earned. This team had never worked on a product for legal and didn't appreciate our concerns around stability and security. This resulted in a standoff, with the development team saying, 'the product is done, we've earned our equity, go sell it,' and I was refusing to take Allegory to market because basic elements were still missing—it was full of bugs and I had no reassurances on its security. We ultimately bought out the development team and raised our first round of financing.

"At that point, believe it or not, my co-founder and I still didn't have our own paperwork, which then became a priority. My co-founder had been one of my best friends, but I quickly learned that starting a business with someone who is reliably down for a good time is not the same as starting a business with someone who is reliable, peri-

od. With a common adversary in the development team, these issues were initially obscured, but they quickly came to the surface and were exacerbated by discussions about rights and responsibilities as we sought to put together our paperwork. Our conflict went on for months, even as the new development team moved forward on stabilizing and improving Allegory and ended in my co-founder suing both me and the company.

"The first two years of Allegory were a crash course in entrepreneurship, software development, and corporate law, but ultimately, the most powerful lessons I learned were about people and perspective, which are what gave me the most strength in the years that followed. As things moved forward, I don't think there was a day running Allegory that I wasn't learning valuable lessons on everything from UX [user experience] design to accounting to fundraising. But the lesson that resonated the most—and continues to resonate—is the power of networking. By nature, I'm an introvert, but it quickly became apparent that I would have to learn to be more extroverted, including finding ways to connect with people who didn't overwhelm my introverted tendencies.

"Shortly after resolving issues with my co-founder, I moved to Silicon Valley, where the power of networking was immediately apparent. I would meet with one person, and, over the course of our conversation, they would think of 10 other people I should meet, and follow that with introductions. At first, I thought this was weird— certainly not something to which I was accustomed as a lawyer at a Big Law firm in New York. But it didn't take long to appreciate how universal this practice was and why. For the first time, it felt like I was moving forward in all the directions I needed to go in order to build the company."

Legal Connection

For a different perspective, Thabo Magubane, a legal tech thought leader and current chief of growth for Legal Connection, a legal tech company, describes his journey into the legal innovation world this way:

> *"South Africa has one of the most progressive democratic constitutions in the world. However, a large majority of people still cannot access the institutions of justice. This sparked a thought in me. Most of the scholars and advocates working on access to justice issues focused solely on legal principles, rather than the physical structures and mechanisms used in the institutions of justice. What I have also noticed and learned in the past years, volunteering and working in legal organizations and law firms, is that there is an existing perception that pro bono means no revenue, and that there also is the 'we have always done it this way' approach, which sometimes led to an unpleasant idea that lawyers existed independently from everyone else. I wouldn't say I liked this; the situation worsened instead of getting better as the years went by.*

> *"Tracing my fascination with technology, primarily health technology, I started connecting with like-minded people searching for something more and became interested in process improvement. I remember vividly some years back when Nonopa Vanda and I presented our research on the use of artificial intelligence and robotics in health care centers at the University of Pretoria, South Africa. As the years went by, I started looking for more information and data-centered research on process improvement. For example, in one of my articles, 'Technology and Law: The Use of Artificial Intelligence and 5G to Access the Courts in Africa' (January 1, 2021), I highlighted an incident that took place in one of the courts in South Africa,*

where a storm damaged the court roof and a large number of essential documents went missing or got damaged. One of the propositions I made was to use technology to supplement existing structures to make them better and more efficient, like cloud computing for storage and other forms of computing powers to ensure security.

"As a legal tech entrepreneur, I am working with and on several start-ups focused on access to justice and helping law firms take more cases at reduced costs while delivering value and generating revenue. Legal technology is an exciting field because of the opportunity it gives legal departments to self-introspect on whether they are doing enough with the resources they have and are there any better ways of doing it available."

Where do we go from here? The journey of change within the law is neither a sprint nor a marathon. It is something more closely akin to an obstacle course. It is challenging, unpredictable, and variable in pace. It is often slow and can be riddled with obstacles to overcome, abrupt starts and stops, and the ever-present potential for failure. The key to getting through is maintaining focus on the goal of making the legal profession what it should always have been: client– and customer-driven.

Chapter 7

Types of Legal Technology

"Contract management tools offer a number of ways to manage the contracting process, but nearly all seek, at the very least, to make contracting a more automated, efficient, and collaborative process."

L EGAL TECHNOLOGY ENCOMPASSES A WIDE RANGE OF types of tools and uses, from document review and workflow management software to cost and litigation analytics. It also encompasses solutions focused on lowering the barriers of entry to the legal industry for those with limited finances or limited knowledge of the legal system in the United States or in other jurisdictions.

One of the oldest areas of legal tech is e-discovery. The Federal Rules of Civil Procedure, the rules governing civil litigation matters in the United States, first mentioned data in 1970.[13]

Electronic discovery is the process in which parties to a lawsuit preserve, review, and share with the other parties to the suit electronically stored information for use as evidence in litigation. Electronically stored information comes in many formats—e-mail, word processing and design applications, spreadsheets, social media messages such as tweets and direct messages, and proprietary databases.

Modern e-discovery tools make extensive use of elements of AI, such as machine learning, to make review of documents more efficient and productive. Some e-discovery companies make use of another element of AI, natural language processing, in which an algorithm detects patterns, trends, and anomalies in ordinary language through the review of large sets of language data. When natural language processing is combined with predictive coding, e-discovery tools cannot only help expedite the review of documents, but also allow for users to derive analytics and potential areas to focus on with respect to their litigation strategy.

ANALYTICS

When most people think about suing someone, they think about it in a fairly direct way, as righting a perceived wrong or injustice. Litigation is far more than that. It is about using facts and persuasion to prove that something illegal happened. Thanks to technology, particularly the use of tools to analyze large sets of data, legal professionals are now able to access tools that analyze litigation patterns and trends that can be invaluable when sketching out a litigation strategy. Use of data (the right data, *i.e.,* a complete and accurate set of data) is critical when relying on such tools.

---

[13] For a brief history of e-discovery, *see* https://zapproved.com/a-timeline-of-electronic-discovery.

Lex Machina

One example of such a company is Lex Machina, which uses algorithm-based "machine learning" and other tools to uncover key insights. These insights support litigation analytics and data used by lawyers and others to help formulate, refine, and execute a variety of litigation strategies.

Lex Machina uses computer science and legal expertise to provide a platform that allows litigators using data-driven analysis to formulate more strategic litigation strategies and potentially win more cases. For example, an attorney could view the total amount of damages awarded by a particular judge in a certain type of case and also compare such data across areas of law or jurisdictions. Answers to questions about the likelihood of a specific motion being granted or how long a case reaches a certain stage can be found using its platform.

UniCourt

Another example is UniCourt. Founder Josh Blandi started the company after a few years running his first company, CountryWide Debt Relief, a high-volume, low-cost legal services model used by law firms to help consumers consolidate and eliminate their debt. UniCourt was started after Blandi realized how difficult it was to get access to trial court data in bulk. The UniCourt platform uses sophisticated data-gathering techniques to collect court data from hundreds of state and federal courts across the United States. UniCourt then makes these data available through application programming interfaces (APIs), which allow two or more computers to communicate. In addition to providing access to this massive database, UniCourt uses AI algorithms to provide a more robust understanding of data trends and statistics. Other functions offered through their API include the automation of time-consuming tasks such as docket data and automatic identification of attorneys, parties, law firms, and judges, along with their associated ongoing litigation matters.

Digitory Legal

Catherine Krow is the founder of Digitory Legal, an award-winning cost analytics platform focused on bringing data-driven pricing and cost prediction to law. Before founding Digitory Legal, Krow practiced law at top-tier firms for 17 years, first at Simpson, Thacher & Bartlett and then at Orrick, Herrinton and Sutcliffe where she was a litigation partner. She was a 2019 American Bar Association Women of Legal Technology List honoree and was included in the FastCase 50 Class of 2019, which honors some of the leading figures in the legal space. I asked her about both her journey into legal technology and about Digitory Legal.

"I was introduced to the entrepreneurial mindset early in my legal career, being part of a team that launched the Silicon Valley office of Simpson Thatcher. As a litigation partner at Orrick, my work involved complex litigation, which led to my interest in scoping, cost management, and then data analytics.

"My desire to solve complex pricing problems coincided with the evolution of the legal profession. Law departments were, and are, under tremendous pressure to reduce budgets and obtain the best value possible from outside counsel. Legal operations and legal procurement have been applying an unprecedented level of business discipline to the legal industry. To succeed in this market, I believed that law firms would need to carefully examine their processes, adopt new technology, and make some significant changes to better meet the business needs of their clients. For me, all this change presented an opportunity to do something new and exciting that would advance the legal profession.

"Digitory's focus is on delivering actionable cost data. By this we mean data with four key attributes: (1) granular enough to reveal scope and unit costs for each task, (2) well labeled, (3) accurately

and consistently coded, and (4) connected to context. We help our customers understand the 'why' behind the numbers, enabling both law firms and legal departments to scope matters and manage costs more efficiently.

"Historically, the legal industry has not been rigorous in its data management practices. This means that we have a lot of data, but the data don't actually tell us anything. In practice, that means that clients are unsure about the value that law firms are delivering, and, in turn, law firms are struggling to demonstrate that value through data. Unless firms tackle the data problem, this disconnect will continue to exist. What we are seeing at Digitory is that when law firms and legal departments clean, analyze, and map their historical data, they see greater profitability, find cost efficiencies, and develop stronger business relationships."

AVOIDING LITIGATION: ALTERNATIVE DISPUTE RESOLUTION

However valuable cost analytics or litigation analytics may be, there are those who will find even greater value in avoiding litigation altogether. Alternative dispute resolution (ADR) covers arbitration, mediation, negotiation, and any other agreed-upon procedure that involves a neutral party who can help the disputants reach agreement and avoid litigation. Although this may not sound like promising territory for legal technology, one experienced arbitrator, Gary Doernhoefer, thinks it is, and he started a firm, ADR Notable, to prove it.

Doernhoefer served as the first general counsel for the travel website, Orbitz, co-founded and served as general counsel for Accertify, Inc. (now a wholly owned subsidiary of American Express), and served as vice president and general counsel through the launch and initial capitalization of Journera, a travel industry technology start-up company. Doernhoefer was for three years general counsel for the International Air Transport Association, the global trade association for the world's airline industry. After three decades of experience managing legal issues and disputes in a wide variety of contexts and helping to launch three start-up companies, he became the founder and managing director of ADR Notable, a leading company in the alternative dispute resolution sector.

Doernhoefer's interest in ADR began during his time with the International Air Transport Association. He explains:

> *"While I was at the International Air Transport Association, I served as an arbitrator in a dispute related to online travel agents and became interested in promoting ADR within the airline industry. ADR is practiced by professionals with titles such as ombudsman, conciliator, or even peacemaker (in Native American culture), as well as the more common titles of mediator or arbitrator. ADR generally has the benefits of resolving a disputed matter confidentially; and in cases that are mediated, there is greater control over the outcome, which is reached by negotiation and mutual agreement instead of judicial fiat.*

> *"My interest in ADR continued after my return to Ohio and I had discussions with the Center for Aviation Studies and the law faculty at the Ohio State University. I took a three-day mediation training workshop led by the university's faculty and noticed the lack of technology in dispute resolution. My entrepreneurial instinct returned, and I began the very first steps toward what is now ADR Notable, LLC—the first technology platform designed specifically for mediators. We were excited when ADR Notable was identified as a 2020 Emerging Legal Technology by the National Law Journal.*

> *"ADR Notable focuses primarily on mediation, in which a third party facilitates discussions and negotiations between parties in conflict.*

Blending technology with mediation requires sensitivity to the methods mediators use. Much of their skill set revolves around uniquely human skills of communication, empathy, trust, and creativity that technology cannot replicate. But the application of those skills takes place in a business context where automation can help.

"We worked very hard to offer a technology that is designed to be intuitive and useful, and to keep it simple where complexity might interfere. For example, we developed a note-taking feature that is simple to use, but offers better organization, sorting, searching, and management than notes on paper. It also allows the mediator to move from typed notes of agreed terms to documentation of the agreement much more easily than retyping handwritten notes. We then surrounded that feature with more common business support tools, such as e-mail and calendar integration, contact management, process flow checklists, document storage and retrieval, secure deletion of confidential materials at the conclusion of cases, and data analytics and reporting across cases. The goal is to offer a complete solution tailored to mediators."

IMPROVING WORKFLOWS

Technology is also addressing one of the thornier problems faced by many legal professionals—managing matters and workflows. Attorneys and others working in the legal arena often carry heavy workloads. Finding a way to keep track of all that goes into such a workload can be painful and time-consuming. Thanks to technological innovation, there are solutions out there that seek to address this very problem. One of the more successful ones is Proxy.

Daniel Farris is a founder of the legal technology firm, Proxy, partner in charge of Norton Rose Fullbright's Chicago office, cofounder of Norton Rose's legal tech subsidiary, LX Studio, and a former software engineer. I spoke with him about his background, about how he balances being a law firm partner and a legal technology firm founder, and about his thoughts on the practice of law. Specifically, I asked why he had thought to start Proxy. Here's what he said:

> *"As an outside lawyer practicing at a large firm, I am fundamentally a service provider. I have been able to observe how the roles, expectations, and stressors affecting my in-house clients have changed over the past 10–15 years. The problem we are trying to solve with Proxy first arose, and quickly became glaring, during the past 10 years or so.*

> *"Providing good client service means more than just protecting my corporate clients' interests. It means understanding the issues that the lawyers working for those corporate clients grapple with every day.*

> *"Perhaps the problem in-house lawyers most often described was the feeling of being hopelessly behind and entirely unable to control and manage their workloads. Some had elaborate spreadsheets. Others had tried third-party tools built for nonlegal functions, mostly without success. Many had simply given up, resigned to prioritize and manage legal tasks by responding to whichever 'high priority' e-mail they received first on any given day.*

> *"As a former software engineer, I was amazed that better legal productivity tools did not exist. I do not fall victim to the belief that technology can solve every problem, but surely it could have an impact on this one. A review of the market showed that most legal tech products were highly segmented, aimed at law firm lawyers, meant to perform single functions (e.g., contracting or docketing), or de-*

signed for narrow substantive legal issues (e.g., real estate or intellectual property).

"What did not exist was a product or platform that was universally available, technology-independent, subject-matter–agnostic, easy, and flexible. Too many products sought to automate tasks for lawyers. We believed (and still do) that giving in-house lawyers intuitive, lightweight, and flexible tools to use as they see fit is the best way to enable and empower a critically underserved market: people, and more precisely, the people who practice law inside corporations.

"Thus the core concepts that today make up the foundation of Proxy's legal workflow management platform were born. Proxy makes it easy for in-house lawyers to organize, track, prioritize, delegate, and report on the tasks, workflows, and projects they manage. Proxy allows for both structured and ad hoc tasks and integrates with e-mail, so in-house lawyers can continue to work the way they already do. The goal of Proxy isn't to replace lawyers or to perform tasks for them, but to empower lawyers to better manage the legal tasks for which they are responsible."

INCREASING ACCESS THROUGH AUTOMATION

Being able to have professional legal help when needed is not entirely a matter of money. There have to be channels for communication, too, and applications that allow clients to connect with attorneys in ways that work for both.

Documate

Dorna Moini is the CEO and a founder of Documate, a no-code platform for building document automation and client-facing legal applications. Before starting Documate, Dorna was a litigator at Sidley Austin. There, in her pro bono practice, she worked with legal aid organizations to build a web application for domestic violence survivors to complete and file their paperwork. This led to the idea for Documate. I asked for her views on document automation and the context for Documate:

> *"Document automation has been around for decades, but Documate is focused on a broader category—the 'productization,' you could call it, of law. On Documate, lawyers can build legal products to generate documents, expert systems, guided interviews, and legal apps. Then they can collaborate with clients online and can generate revenue through new legal service delivery models. More important, lawyers can build these products on their own. Documate offers the power of functions such as loops, complex calculations, and nested logic—with the ease and user experience of a modern, no-code platform.*

> *"Our roots are in legal aid, but even the for-profit law firms that use Documate are building tools that increase access to legal services. We first built Documate to allow clinical programs at legal aid organizations to scale their impact. For example, one of the first users was a legal aid organization with way more demand for its Saturday morning eviction defense clinics than it could support. So it built a tool on Documate and served more than 10 times the number of people it had served through direct client contact. We now work with schools, court systems, government entities, and law firms to build scalable legal tech tools that allow these organizations to provide more affordable services."*

SixFifty

Another story of legal technology increasing access to justice is the powerful example of SixFifty. Kimball Parker is the founder of SixFifty, director of the Legal Design Clinic at Brigham Young University, and a former attorney who founded the innovation subsidiary of the law firm, Parsons Behle & Latimer. His passion and dedication to making the legal system more accessible and less costly is evident in all that he has achieved. Parker shared the story of SixFifty with me.

> "LawX, now known as the Legal Design Clinic, at Brigham Young University came before SixFifty (a technology company that is dedicated to making the law more accessible) and helped inspire it. The idea behind LawX was to work with students to pick an area of law that people struggle with when they can't afford an attorney, and to develop a software solution to that problem within a single semester. The first year we picked debt collection and we built a program, SoloSuit, to help people respond to a debt collection lawsuit. We released the product after the semester and we had more users in a month than we had expected in an entire year. More than 7,000 people have used that tool. The next year we collaborated with the University of Arizona to address evictions, and we built an automated tool that helps people write their landlords when they can't pay rent, called HelloLandlord. After launch, we made HelloLandlord a part of SixFifty so the product could have the engineering and legal support it needed. During the pandemic, we adjusted HelloLandlord to account for the federal and local eviction moratoriums.

> "SixFifty came on the heels of the success of LawX. Wilson Sonsini Goodrich & Rosati wanted to automate legal documents for businesses, and LawX caught the firm's eye. This attention excited me because Wilson Sonsini is one of the best business and IP law firms in the world. If we could take its top-tier expertise and plug it into

automation tools, we could make high-quality legal help more accessible and affordable for everyone—for people and businesses. We've initially focused our efforts in privacy and employment law, and have succeeded in both areas. We recently released an automated employee handbook that has become SixFifty's best-selling product to date."

MANAGING CONTRACTS

Too often contracts are conflated with contracts management. Contracts themselves are legal documents and, accordingly, are drafted and negotiated by legal professionals. Managing those contracts, however, is a different matter involving multiple functions far beyond the legal department. This has not gone unnoticed by those in the legal tech space. Legal technology designed to be used in contract management (also called contract lifecycle management, or CLM) is one of the most prominent types of legal technology and one that has attracted a massive amount of investment. Perhaps this is because contracts form the foundation on which nearly all businesses are built and then grow.

As the complexity of businesses has grown, so has the complexity, and the number and types, of contracts that are needed. Businesses have always needed to manage contracts and the contracting process, *e.g.*, who has to review a contract, what parts of the contract have to be reviewed, who has to approve a contract, how to track contract deadlines, and so on. However, management has become a time-consuming and complex task that requires the attention and work of far more than just a legal department.

Poor management of agreements can lead to wasted time, decreased productivity, and more room for error. Effective contract management can enable the streamlining and automating of both managing agreements and creating new ones. A legal tech solution can also help control costs, oversee payments and other key contractual obligations, and reduce room for error. Consider the fact that a study by PricewaterhouseCoopers concluded that contract management can potentially reduce negotiation cycles by more than half and cut operating costs of managing agreements by up to 30 percent.[14]

To accommodate this increase in complexity, a large number of companies have developed products that are dedicated to managing contracting from negotiation through drafting, execution, performance, and reporting. As the number of companies in contract management has grown and their successes have been noticed, investors have poured money into the space.

Contract management tools offer several ways to manage the contracting process, but nearly all seek, at the very least, to make contracting a more automated, efficient, and collaborative process. Examples of companies offering contract management solutions include Malbek, Ironclad, Juro, and Agiloft.

I spoke with Matt Patel, one of the co-founders of Malbek, who shared the following about what led to the start of Malbek:

> *"I started my career as a computer engineer out of college; I enjoyed programming and building software. It was good to get that exposure on how technology is built, but I soon realized I am more of a customer-facing guy. I enjoyed talking to clients, understanding their use cases, and translating that to an R&D team to build custom solutions that solve those challenges. In 2006, I switched to a small organization that had a suite of packaged software solutions. One of them was a tool designed to help organizations with their contract lifecycle management needs. I was no expert, with zero experience in this space. But one thing college taught me is how to learn. It didn't take long for me to build expertise in CLM and become a primary contact for all our CLM customers. I built strong relationships with customers, partners, and the analyst community. However, the product was quite old and couldn't keep up with innovation; it was losing traction. I saw firsthand what customers are trying to achieve*

---

[14] Andy Coaton, "Contract Management: Control Value and Minimise Risks," White Paper, PricewaterhouseCoopers, 2003.

with a CLM solution, and what is working and what is not working. The company was acquired in 2016. I was fortunate to get a chance to build a new CLM solution, the right way from the ground up, with my amazing co-founders and a team of determined individuals that brought the right mindset, right vision, and right experience. Welcome to Malbek."

I also asked Matt about some of the more commonly misunderstood aspects of contract management solutions. He said:

"There are a few aspects of CLM that are misunderstood. CLM is still often considered to be a legal department tool, which is not the case; it should be considered an enterprise tool. CLM is still considered to be a single solution; it should be considered to be a platform in your technology stack. CLM use cases are spread across the entire lifecycle of the contract from cradle to grave, but there are still many solutions that address only one or two use cases in contract management but claim to be CLM solutions. A true CLM application needs to be a platform, with end-to-end capabilities, with AI infused across the entire contract journey and not just one or two use cases. It should manage post-signature processes and it should be easily integrated with customer relationship management tools, MS Office, collaboration tools such as Microsoft Teams or Slack, and other tools in the enterprise technology stack at every organization. I believe the reason for some of these misunderstandings is that there are a lot of products in the market and the marketing for each stretches the truth and confuses the buyer. There is only a handful of true CLM platforms that are leading the industry; the number is in the single digits."

Chapter 8

Teaching Legal Technology

"As with learning to use any tool, one of the first things to do is learn what the tool is used for and then try using it for that defined purpose."

THERE'S A LONG-STANDING JOKE THAT YOU GO TO LAW school to avoid math. The joke now could be that you go to law school to avoid data and technology. Unfortunately, avoiding technology is the opposite of what lawyers need to do to succeed in a world that is ever more dependent on technology, in which technology governs more and more of how we live.

When the topic of teaching law students or lawyers something technology-related arises, the subject of coding inevitably comes up. I am not a programmer. In fact, back in college, I had a fear of computer science because I had a fear of mathematics and I saw the two as inexorably linked. I didn't like math until I took my first class in economics. Once I saw mathematical concepts in the context of something else, I saw how computer science and programming are not so much about math as they are about creating new things—things that could help people be more productive, more efficient, and more focused on things that matter and less on things that don't.

TEACHING THE CONCEPTS

This is what teaching legal technology to law students is all about. It's not about learning to be a programmer or a data geek; it's not about a specific piece of technology at all. It is about teaching law students (and lawyers) about technological concepts that will come into play as they practice law or support others who do.[15] Specific technologies can and do change rapidly. The concepts underlying technological tools do not change nearly as quickly, which is why teaching the concepts and not specific tools makes more sense.

As Gabriel H. Teninbaum, currently serving as assistant dean of Innovation, Strategic Initiatives and Distance Education, at Suffolk University Law School, notes, "I think every legal professional should have an understanding of the relevant technologies to their practice areas, and to make smart decisions about when to use them. Part and parcel of that is having a broad understanding of what coding is and what sorts of problems it's capable of solving (and, just as important, what problems it's not capable of solving)."

The question of teaching legal technology to law students and lawyers, though, is not only about technological concepts or coding. It is also about aligning the legal profession to the needs of people living in a dynamic and evolving world. To answer the question of how to align the legal profession to the needs of legal services consumers, Teninbaum says the following:

"I'll limit my answer to Suffolk Law, where we work very hard to

help achieve alignment. Beyond the traditional courses and a huge

---

[15] "Technology does not exist in a vacuum. It needs to be applied to something to actually work and then people have to actually leverage it to do work." Sharon D. Nelson and Jim Calloway, "Professor Kenton Brice on Training the Next Generation of Lawyers and the Future of Legal Tech," Legal Talk Network, June 16, 2022.

catalog of electives, we also give students as many valuable experiences as we can to supplement what they learn in the classroom. For example, in a typical year, something like a hundred of our 1Ls spend the summer as judicial interns in Massachusetts courts. They get an up-close-and-personal perspective on litigation while being mentored by a judge. Suffolk has unique programs, such as the Accelerator-to-Practice Program, which is the first of its kind. It is a comprehensive three-year course of study and practice designed to prepare graduates to join or start sustainable law practices serving average-income individuals and families. Also, on the cutting-edge end of things, we have the nation's #1 ranked legal technology program, per National Jurist *magazine. We are focused on showing students how to deliver legal services in new ways and to be competitive for legal jobs with titles that didn't even exist 20 years ago (our alums' titles include 'legal solutions architect,' 'innovation consultant,' 'legal project manager,' and more). Plus, the school has invested in significant ways to align its more traditional programs with law practice. For example, Suffolk Law has legal writing, clinical, and ADR programs ranked in the top 25 programs nationally."*

Aligning the delivery of legal services to the needs of legal consumers requires meeting legal consumers where they are. For sophisticated legal consumers, this means speaking the language of business—which is the language of data and numbers. Someone who continues to make strides in this area is Professor Daniel Katz.

Professor Katz is a scientist, technologist, and professor who applies an innovative polytechnic approach to teaching law with the aim of helping to create lawyers who can meet today's biggest societal challenges. His scholarship and his teaching integrate science, technology, engineering, and mathematics. Professor Katz is well-known for his work in legal informatics, which the American Library Association defines as being "the study of the structure and properties of information, as well as the application of technology to the organization, storage, retrieval, and dissemination of information."

I spoke with Professor Katz about lawyers' perceived fear of mathematics and data, and about how law schools can better prepare their students to practice law now. He thinks the perception is real, and law schools will have to adjust:

> *"I don't think that they are pretending—I do think that they are truly afraid of mathematics and data. But, to be a lawyer, you need to be whatever it is you need to be. That is to say, you need to be able to attain the skills required to do your job and give your client what your client wants. Lawyers can do math, they just fear it, and they need to face that fear and overcome it if they want to practice law in the 21st century.*

> *"Law schools have taught certain things, the teaching of which hasn't changed in 10 years, 20 years, even 50 years. They do a good job of teaching those basic standard subjects—take torts, for example. But law schools have a difficult time teaching law from a multidisciplinary perspective, teaching those skills that supplement your legal abilities, teaching design thinking, analytics, project management. These are things that law schools have not taught before. The 21st-century lawyer needs to have this kind of polytechnic background. Being a lawyer is about being far more than just a substantive expert. To use but one example, smart contracts will start to have a big impact on how lawyers practice. Instead of knowing simply how to write, then, lawyers will also need to know how to read code."*

David Colarusso, the director of Suffolk University Law School's Legal Innovation and Technology Lab, notes: "Digital technology has changed law in the same ways that other technologies have, which is to say that it's made certain things easier, and it's made the ability to scale your work easier in some respects."[16]

It's this ability to scale that makes learning how to read or write code, or both, can be useful for lawyers. The goal for learning to read code is to achieve a specific outcome. By knowing how to read code, a lawyer can more fully recognize the boundaries of what is possible and potentially develop his or her own solution to a problem. As with learning to use any tool, one of the first things to do is learn what the tool is used for and then try using it for that defined purpose.

ANTICIPATING CHANGE

Despite both the fear many have about using technology and the contrived misgivings of some in the legal profession about teaching legal technology and preparing students for practice in the 21st century, many others are not content with waiting for this to change. Quddus Pourshafie is one of those people.

Currently director at NFTUX, Quddus Pourshafie is an educator and legal technology founder who developed what he calls the Future Framework for Legal Practice (FFLP). He designed it to be

> *"a means to educate lawyers, helping them understand what is needed to prepare and build a future-facing firm. One application is as a conceptual framework, something that allows a reader to understand how technology might fit into one or more areas of their practice of law to begin practically compartmentalizing and applying readily available technology to their firm. Another application is in the way the framework elicits a type of systems thinking approach to transformation and agility in the direction the leaders of the firm take, in terms of what their main type of workload may be and what other industries they will closer align to and service.*

---

[16] Sharon Miki, "Programming for Lawyers: Why Lawyers Make Good Programmers," Clio Technology Posts, n.d.

"The FFLP is needed predominantly because every great piece of technology or innovation that comes about will toot its own horn. On a grand scale, this is great for the fundamental changes in the legal industry, but for a managing partner, it doesn't solve the issue of how that piece of technology fits in with everything else. This is exacerbated when multiple potential technologies that service different processes of the firm are being considered. Essentially, legal technology was initially built to service niche areas of the traditional partnership model, but over time, legal tech has matured to a point where it considers other models of operation entirely. There is no framework that helps make sense of the exponential growth and maturation of legal technology and how legal technology fits into a business model for legal services now and in the future. This is the rationale for the FFLP and why it exists."

Some law schools, such as Suffolk University Law School, Northeastern Law School, Northwestern Pritzker School of Law, and Stanford Law School, have taken heed of what individuals like Quddus have attempted to do. Both Suffolk and Northwestern, for example, offer robust legal technology curricula; Suffolk also offers an online certificate program in legal tech for professionals. Stanford has CodeX—the Stanford Center for Legal Informatics—where "researchers, lawyers, entrepreneurs, and technologists work side-by-side to advance the frontier of legal technology, bringing new levels of legal efficiency, transparency, and access to legal systems around the world."[17]

Peter Lederer spent 70 years within the legal industry, served both as a partner of a major law firm and as general counsel of a global corporation, and was well-known as a forward-thinking teacher, leader, and lawyer. To many, including me, he was an icon and a beacon of hope within the legal industry who spent decades thinking about and actively trying to align legal education with the needs of

---

[17] *See* Codex: The Stanford Center for Legal Informatics. Overview.

today's consumers of legal services. I was lucky to have spoken with him before his untimely death about this question of alignment and his assessment of the progress made so far. He offered this perspective:

> "If the way in which legal services are being delivered is undergoing rapid change (think LegalZoom, DoNotPay, UnitedLex, the Big Four accounting firms, and a multitude more), then surely the way we educate those who are to deliver legal services is also undergoing change, no? The answer, unfortunately, is well, yes—but only at a glacial pace. In this country, only a handful of law schools—perhaps 10 percent or so of the 200 accredited schools—have even as much as a single program that meaningfully explores and trains students for the so-called New Law. Miami Law's Michele DeStefano and Law-WithoutWalls, Indiana's Bill Henderson and his Institute for the Future of Law Practice, and Vanderbilt's Cat Moon and her Program in Law and Innovation are shining examples of these rare exceptions. That is clearly not enough, and legal education as we know it faces an existential crisis. So yes, it has a lot of catching up to do. Whether it can, and whether it has the will to do so, are very much open questions.

> "For several years the American Bar Association's Commission on the Future of Legal Education has been hard at work at finding a path forward. It's like the old light-bulb joke: 'How many psychiatrists does it take to change a light bulb? It only takes one—but the bulb really has to want to change!' It's too early to predict the outcome. I am convinced, however, that the emerging legal service providers will not long be prepared to pay—directly or indirectly—for the embedded costs of our legal education edifice."

Jeff Carr describes himself as a legal rebel, a description I agree with. He has spent more than 30 years fighting for change within the legal industry, most recently as general counsel for several large companies, including Univar Solutions. Before this, and after retiring as general counsel of FMC in 2014, Carr worked with Valorem Law, one of the earliest law firms to focus on making alternative fee arrangements the norm. Valorem served as the basis for ElevateNext, the law firm affiliate of the global law company, Elevate. When not pushing for change, he is an active race car driver.

I asked Carr how he thought lawyers should be prepared for the increasingly digital world of law practice. He thinks a change of perspective is needed:

> "I'm not so focused on training for the increasingly digital world, that will simply come as the tools—the platforms—in use arise, change, and are replaced in a natural cycle of innovation and adoption. What I am focused on is how to educate lawyers and prepare them to be focused on customers instead of on the profession. After all, the legal ecosystem exists to serve only two purposes: for individual customers (whether a person or corporation, as both are subject to and beneficiaries of the rule of law) and for society as a customer at large (creator of the rule of law). This requires a sea change in perspective and focus. We have to abandon the quest for excellence and the answers to interesting questions of law and instead focus on what the customer truly needs.

> "As Richard Susskind famously observed, Black & Decker's customers don't want a drill, they want a hole in the wall. In #lawland, few, if any, customers want litigation or problems. They want to grow their businesses responsibly, safely, and profitably. Increasingly, they also want to 'do good' for all stakeholders, including employees and communities as well as shareholders; in other words, they want responsible revenue acceleration. This requires the legal

profession to change its focus to the customer, to actually delivering value. This means truly understanding the customer's needs and objectives and then providing a delivered-value service that results in effectiveness (objective achieved), efficiency (on or under the agreed budget by using only those resources needed), and a good experience (for the customer, not the provider). At the end of the day, our purpose, and everything we do, every single day, has to come down to this delivered-value model. This is the Way."

Many of the innovators and legal industry leaders I have spoken with over the years have had an opinion (or opinions) on legal education. When I spoke with Jordan Furlong, we returned to the beginning: are there too many lawyers, too many law schools, or too many of both? His response was in accord with Dan Katz's:

"There are too many law schools teaching law in the old way, producing too many lawyers who think and act in the old way. We don't need any more of either; as it happens, market forces are in action to cull both those herds, so this problem will solve itself in due course. What we don't really have yet, and what I don't see enough of on the immediate horizon, is law schools that prepare lawyers who can deliver value in the 21st century. There are some exceptions (including Suffolk Law) to that rule—but, frustratingly, they're still exceptions.

"I don't entirely blame the law schools. I place the real responsibility on the legal profession's regulators, who should be setting minimum standards of postgraduate competence and refusing to admit to practice any new graduate who doesn't meet them. I don't mean the bar exam, which is, I'm sorry, a joke. Would you trust your life to a doctor who had only to pass a certifying test similar to the bar exam? I mean a thorough, multidisciplinary, practical, and assessable

standard of minimum competence to provide reliable services of value to clients. The United Kingdom has developed such a standard. Canada has developed such a standard. Not one U.S. state, as far as I can tell, even has one in the works.

"Give law schools a new standard of achievement for their graduates to meet and refuse to admit to practice any graduate who doesn't meet it. Many law schools will shut down, unable to adjust to that new standard. Many others will adjust and start producing lawyers who can provide value upon graduation. And many new providers will emerge to fill that role. That's how to fix legal education."

The world is a dynamic place. It does not make sense that those seeking to address the needs of those living in this world should be trained in a vacuum or be trained that there is just one way of doing something. In some ways, the legal industry is at a stage of development that another once-resistant-to-change profession—the medical profession—used to be. For many generations, the treatment of patients was done one way and that was it. Technology then came along and has transformed not only how patients are treated, but also the treatments that are available.

The legal industry is finally starting to realize the power of technology to influence not just existing lawyers, but would-be lawyers, and also how they are trained prior to entering the profession. And it is not just technology that is impacting the training of lawyers, but the pace of change in the world—a pace that continues to accelerate.

Chapter 9

Leading Through Change: A Tale of Collaboration and Empathy

"So, what are the key values of leaders who can successfully navigate the choppy waters of today? The top three are easy to state and much harder to practice."

C OLLABORATION IS A PROCESS OF EXCHANGING IDEAS, learning from one another, and taking that shared learning to create something new. It requires communication skills, trust (built on responses that are reliable), flexibility, and emotional intelligence, particularly when it comes to managing stress.

Collaboration is not a technology, but—as has been made all too plain through the COVID-19 pandemic—it is something greatly assisted by technology. This appears in the widespread use of software, from the near-ubiquitous Microsoft Office (documents) and Zoom (videoconferencing) to contract automation and electronic signatures.

SERVING CLIENTS

Quinten Steenhuis of Greater Boston Legal Services explicitly directs his technological work there to "scripting, automation, and monitoring to build a reliable system that encourages collaboration and facilitates the service of our client population." Another example of collaborative technology that addresses a problem is the Florida Bar's Florida Pro Bono Matters, which, says Eli Mattern, "showcases available pro bono opportunities in Florida. The cases are posted by legal services programs all over the state so that attorneys can shop for cases that interest them." Eli Mattern is chief executive officer of SavvySuit, which develops software to increase access to justice as well as products for the private bar.

One important element of collaboration is the management of various projects. Traditionally, lawyers have not been good at project management. The reason is seemingly simple—they have not been taught how, nor have they been taught its importance. Yet, in the professional world, we all are given projects of varying complexity and length, and completing them often requires the support and input of others not directly assigned to that project. One individual who can speak directly to this is Larry Bridgesmith.

Larry Bridgesmith is adjunct professor of law at Vanderbilt University Law School and a leading voice in the legal innovation space. He has more than 30 years of experience in the dispute resolution field. He also co-founded LPM Alignment, which is the first approved training program in the United States for the certification program of the International Institute for Legal Project Management. He has decided ideas about what lawyers need to know and collaboration are at the top of his list:

> *"Lawyers didn't need to learn to pilot aircraft to travel across the country to get to a distant deposition. Lawyers didn't need to learn how to install phone equipment to improve client communication.*

Lawyers don't have to become CPAs to make sure their accounts and tax filings are accurate.

"Instead, lawyers need to know how to work with many different disciplines and professionals in order to provide their legal services excellently, on time, and at prices clients are willing to pay. They may find it helpful to know the basics of electricity, the principles of hydraulics, or the fundamentals of biology, chemistry, and math. However, excellent lawyers have never had to be (and will never have to be) experts in everything. That is simply not possible. As much as I would like to fly a plane, obtain a Ph.D. in neuroscience, or understand quantum physics, I can be a great lawyer without those added credentials.

"Computer system engineers, data analysts, architects, and software developers are highly valued professionals. As helpful as it may be to know the basics of how to code, legal proficiency doesn't require it. A lawyer's ethical responsibility is to stay abreast of technology developments, not master them.

"As a lawyer, I am better served by avoiding our profession's tendency to divide the world into two separate populations. Just as there are no non-doctors, non-plumbers, or non-TV personalities, there should be no non-lawyers. There are lawyers, and there are all the other careers, professionals, and technical skills on which attorneys depend to practice law."

Susan Hackett is CEO of Legal Executive Leadership, LLC, which is a recognized leader in building smarter and better legal practices. She helps her clients change behaviors, improve operational processes, drive demonstrable client results, and move confidently from traditional practice toward legal executive leadership. I asked her for her thoughts on innovation as it relates to the changes taking place within the legal industry. Her response emphatically emphasizes values as driving the aptitude and pace of change:

> *"I am not a fan of using the word 'innovation' in my practice or in describing the movement going on today. I think the better focus is on leadership as a distinguishing trait we wish to promote, and not on innovation. I also value the concepts of inclusiveness and collaboration on legal teams above the concept of innovation. Far too often, lawyers have overlooked, disrespected, or discounted the value of other experiences and disciplines in the better delivery of client services and results. Because clients have real-life business problems, not 'legal' problems, they need real-life teams who can collaborate to provide business solutions, not an insular legal analysis of the issue."*

LEADING A TEAM

Nearly all the conversations I have had with some of the legal industry's most forward-thinking leaders reflect Susan Hackett's emphasis on leadership, inclusiveness, and collaboration.

Mitch Kowalski, for example, is a leader in legal innovation. He has spent more than 25 years in a variety of roles in the legal space, as a lawyer, writer, and professor, and is the author of the critically acclaimed books, *Avoiding Extinction: Reimagining Legal Services for the 21st Century* and *The Great Legal Reformation: Notes From the Field*. My question about how to manage legal processes better in today's environment led to a discussion on leadership:

> *"Legal processes can be better managed by creating a proprietary mix of people, processes, and technologies. Truly innovative legal providers will scale up, not by hiring more lawyers, but by increasing the number of opportunities for team members who have no interest in taking bar exams. These firms will see lawyers as just one*

piece of the puzzle, instead of the entire puzzle. They will understand the value of continuous process improvement—a disciplined approach to critically and continually assessing what is being done and why, to reduce timelines, improve quality, and provide more cost-effective legal services. And they will view it as not a cost-cutting measure, but as a smarter and better use of talent.

"All of this leads to a question that will be distressing in itself to many lawyers. If some legal work can be performed solely by technology and other portions can be performed by team members supported by technology, process, and workflow, how many lawyers does a law firm really need? And who should really be managing and leading such a firm? In a corporate model, the client's experience does not revolve around a specific person; everyone on the team is important, but no one is that important."

Varun Mehta of Factor, Kenny Robertson of the Royal Bank of Scotland (RBS), and Dennis Garcia of Microsoft embody the empathetic leadership style alluded to by both Mitch and Susan. They variously describe their work as engaging people, supporting collaboration, accepting failure as an inherent part of the growth process, and embracing the ideas and encouraging the exchange of ideas from other disciplines.

Varun Mehta is the chief executive officer of Factor (formerly Axiom Managed Solutions), a leader in handling large volumes of highly complex legal work. Emblematic of this is the fact that Factor serves more than 50 of the Fortune 500 or FTSE 100 companies, combining the legal skill, market know-how, and expertise of traditional law with the process efficiency, technology, and data orientation of New Law. A long-time problem-solver and biomedical engineer by training, Varun is a trusted advisor to general counsel and legal operations leaders within global organizations. His efforts have helped legal departments innovate, transformed how legal work is delivered, and generated value across the legal landscape. In his work at Factor, he emphasizes leadership by engagement:

> *"Something I'm focused on at Factor is engaging our people. They are some of the most passionate, driven, knowledgeable people around. I work to create the best culture for them, one where they love what they do and can believe in our mission. It's those people who will drive innovation.*

> *"I also work to build community. We won't solve problems being insular. We need to bring great thinkers from other markets, and we need to unlock great thinkers from our own world to solve bigger problems. We need to enable as many of those wanting to start big ideas by funding start-ups as investors, trying new services for clients, and helping as advisors.*

> *"One thing I admired Axiom for a great deal was its ability to bring tremendously bright minds into our market from outside the industry. Mark Harris, founder of Axiom, is on the board at Factor. He talks about some amazing employees—former leaders, consultants, or engineers who were solving problems in other markets and industries, and were excited to join the wild world of legal with Axiom and transform it for the better."*

Kenny Robertson is head of the Outsourcing, Technology, and Intellectual Property legal team at RBS. He has led some of the largest technology outsourcing projects in the United Kingdom and is additionally responsible for the bank's roll out and adoption of legal technology. I asked him how, in his experience, collaboration and people fit into solving problems with technology. He had evidently been thinking about this:

> *"I think a key enabler for innovation (among other things) is getting the culture right. We have invested time in thinking about what*

kind of team we are, what kind of team we want to be, and how we might get there. As a result, we've boiled down our culture to three 'pillars,' one of which relates to promoting a progressive mindset. Central to this is trying to identify innovation wherever it arises, and trying it out it within the team.

"As an example, for a couple of years, we've been working with design thinking. In and of itself, design thinking has benefited the team through using empathy to develop a better understanding of issues and creating a platform for ideation and prototyping. It's also aligned us far more with our innovation stakeholders, who work with design thinking on a daily basis. Being able to hold a conversation about double diamonds and so on has made us a much more interesting support team! It's also been fun and has democratized the team; there's a palpable energy at an ideation session, and being able to crowdsource ideas from a group of bright people produces far richer answers than anything any one of us would produce on our own.

"We've also made a point of taking advantage of the wealth of content from thought leaders that is now available online and through podcasts. Professor Cat Moon is someone I've gotten to know a bit since I first met her at a conference in Toronto a couple of years ago. I admire Cat, and we've adopted much of her work on failure camp. Introducing and putting a premium on psychological safety has underpinned the culture we have as a team, bringing an openness and an acceptance that, although we'll always do our best, sometimes things will go wrong, and it's okay to share failure. Piercing the notion of lawyerly perfection has helped our focus on well-being, and through sharing 'intelligent failure,' supported the bank's drive to sustain a generative risk culture.

"We also have made a point of being curious about how other industries operate. We've looked at how aviation and health care have used psychological safety to mitigate risk, and how each industry has used basic checklists to elevate performance levels. We've explored how third parties have used techniques such as behavioral economics or nudge theory to exert influence, and looked at what we can learn from how marketers go about understanding and prioritizing customer experience.

"I think it's important to be clear on what levels you must proactively collaborate and generate perspectives that are as broad as possible. Law firms sit across a disparate range of clients that are generating insights about market trends, which can be a rich source of ideas and inspiration. There must be an investment of time and effort on both sides to understand the value in this, if you can be open with firms about what your strategy, culture, and priorities are. What insights you can glean from other firms can be a differentiator.

"Critically, we know we won't always get it right, but going back to the culture argument, we have a platform where prototyping new ideas is welcomed and supported, even when they sometimes don't deliver what we'd hoped. I think it's always going to be an uphill struggle to innovate meaningfully within any team where a positive, progressive culture is absent."

A shining example of how innovation and technology can go hand in hand is when it comes to supporting a dynamic, large, and fast-paced sales team. Dennis Garcia, who leads such a team at Microsoft, explains his life at the intersection of law, technology, and business.

Dennis Garcia is a legal leader at one of the world's most recognized companies. Dennis serves as the lead lawyer for three large business units that are part of Microsoft U.S. (the primary U.S. sales and marketing entity of Microsoft) (1) Global & Partner Solutions (formerly known as One Commercial Partner); (2) Chief Digital Officer; and (3) Marketing and Operations. Garcia's work supports nearly 2,000 professionals. He is active on social media and writes an award-winning blog, *In-House Consigliere*, about the practice of law. I asked him about his work.

> *"I lead a team of 14 outstanding legal professionals located across the United States. We provide legal support to more than 2,000 sales and technical professionals who are part of our U.S. Enterprise Commercial segment—one of Microsoft's largest businesses. My team and I spend time shaping and negotiating a variety of contractual arrangements with our customers and providing general legal support to our business clients on a wide range of issues.*

> *"There are a few ways I try to innovate. First, it all starts with embracing the 'growth mindset' in everything I do. I do my best to absorb as much information as I can about our business, our technology solutions, our customers, our competitors, and the fast-changing intersection of technology and the law. When I make mistakes, I try to learn from them; I don't dwell on my mistakes, and I move forward.*

> *"Another way I try to innovate is by embracing empathy. As a lawyer in the trenches with our sales and technical professionals, it's important for me to be customer-centric—toward our business clients, our end-user customers, and my own team. Appreciating and being empathetic to their perspectives means I am better positioned to be a pragmatic, proactive, and innovative problem-solver by developing smart risk-taking solutions that align with the needs of both Microsoft and Microsoft's customers."*

So, what are the key values of leaders who can successfully navigate the choppy waters of today? The top three are easy to state and much harder to practice:

1. Collaboration—a willingness and desire to incorporate the ideas of others through a shared approach to working together and to executing ideas.

2. Cross-disciplinary learning—accepting the input of those outside the discipline or industry and applying that input to current and future initiatives.

3. Empathy—being able to both see and relate to things as seen through the eyes of others and understanding their motivations for working the way they work.

Chapter 10

Managing People and Managing Change

"However resistant to change lawyers might be, sooner or later the inevitable occurs, and they must deal with it in one way or another."

MANAGING PEOPLE AND CHANGE IS NOT EASY; OFTEN, it is one of the hardest things to do in life. Consider that once our ancestors had found a way to survive, they might have had no need to find a new way if the current way worked well enough.

Fast forward to the modern day: When I first moved out of my parents' house and into a friend's one-bedroom apartment, it was not easy. I had a lot of stuff—and I now was sharing this much smaller space with another human and a cat. Accommodating these new parts of my life required much adaptation and flexibility. I managed to adapt, but it took time and it required me to learn about the needs of the others I was living with.

Now consider law school, where law students are taught a specific way to think, to act, and to analyze, and where there was little talk, let alone use, of technology, except for LexisNexis and Westlaw. Then consider asking or requiring lawyers to be open to considering alternatives to how they were taught to think and act. That is a tall order and one that takes the right mix of incentives, dedication, and time.

Add to this the rise of new technological tools to be used in legal work, including the use of data and statistics—two things that may have been the reason for going to law school instead of business school in the first place! A genuine challenge is presented to those seeking to get the legal industry to embrace change, and more specifically, to embrace technology. Someone who knows these challenges all too well is Dan Currell.

CHANGE IS HARD

Dan Currell is an experienced lawyer, management consultant, and legal innovation leader. He currently serves as senior advisor within the Office of Finance and Operations at the U.S. Department of Education. I had the pleasure of speaking with him about his background, his insights, and his views on the current state of legal technology. Here is what he said:

> *"After law school, I spent two years doing general commercial litigation. Like a lot of my law school classmates, I was writing law review articles in my so-called spare time. My friends were in the job market to become law professors, but that wasn't my direction. In 1999, I went to a management consultancy called the Corporate Executive Board, where my main responsibility was to deliver research presentations to corporate executive teams, mostly at larger public companies. Throughout law school I had been more naturally interested in law and economics than pure doctrinal law, and as a young*

practicing lawyer I was terrified by the process inefficiency of, well, everything. So management consulting was the right move for me.

"For 15 years, I was working with corporate general counsel (in the General Counsel Roundtable), chief compliance officers, chief risk officers, chief privacy officers, and other groups, such as human resources, corporate real estate, tax, finance, and the like. I did around 800 presentations, worked with thousands of companies, worked on every continent. It was a lifetime in 15 years. If that sounds like an exaggeration—it was just how the business model worked. We touched everyone. As to insights—we were in the insight business, so there's more to say there than I can put in a paragraph. But here are three big ones:

"One, execution is incredibly hard in large organizations, and everyone up and down the line has a defensible reason not to change how they do things. Strong leaders are persistent, and they just push through that resistance. That said, most leaders don't really try—and that is far more true with general counsel than with, e.g., chief information officers or other senior executives. Lawyers tend to be deferential to their teams, valuing collegiality above efficiency. That's got a lot of value of its own, but it makes innovation and improvement in the legal sector much harder.

"Two, nobody is asking the general counsel of a large organization to change—not the chief executive officer, not the chief financial officer, certainly not the board, and rarely her direct reports. The general counsel must have the drive to improve things and has to stick with that drive in the absence of support from anywhere. This is why it's easy to start change initiatives in legal but nearly impossible to finish them.

"Three, another leading reason why legal organizations don't change is a lack of existing processes. Process is architecture, and you can't change your plans if you don't have any. To stick with the architecture analogy—lawyers like to just go out and start laying bricks; they'll design the thing (whether it's a transaction, litigation, compliance, whatever) as they go. There are rational reasons for this, but the bottom line is that if you want to change something, you need to know what it is now. Lawyers evade change at the outset by denying that there even is a process that's there to be changed. And they're right. They are just out there laying bricks. If you want to fix that process—where do you even start? It's like trying to carry someone who is passed out. Even a small person—she's just boneless, you've got nothing to hang onto. And if it's a football player, God help you. The rest of the team can't haul him, it's like trying to carry a giant squid—or reform a big due diligence process."

Thinking about process in terms of putting together pieces or as planning out a house is an apt way to also describe another quickly rising area within the legal tech ecosystem, which is legal operations. One of the leaders in legal operations is Mary O'Carroll.

PROCESS IS ARCHITECTURE: LEGAL OPERATIONS

Dan Currell's point that process is architecture, and you can't change a process if you don't have any—at least, any that are acknowledged—would sound familiar to Mary O'Carroll, who, as a co-founder of the Corporate Legal Operations Consortium, or CLOC, was one of the first to make the idea of, and need for, legal operations well known. She explained why legal operations is an important function:

"'Legal operations' describes a set of business processes, activities, and the professionals who enable legal organizations to serve their

clients more effectively by applying business and technical practices to the delivery of legal services. The legal operations function includes things such as strategic planning, financial management, project management, and technology expertise—all things that enable legal professionals to focus on providing legal advice. This is important because it allows a legal department to do three things well: execute at scale, optimize resources and value through efficient sourcing, and improve clients' experiences.

"It is hard for me to imagine how a legal department can survive today without an operations unit. Legal operations is also important because it has been the main driver of transformation in the legal industry. Legal operations professionals are laser focused on efficiency and effectiveness; they created and are driving a demand in the industry for better pricing models, alternative legal services providers, legal technology, data analytics, project management, and so on. That, in turn, has created new roles and job functions throughout the legal ecosystem. This has already had an impact on legal education and training, because the lawyers of tomorrow will be practicing law in different ways that require more collaboration, more technical skills, and more data analysis than needed in the past. Graduates of law schools who once only had one path to follow now have a plethora of options and directions to choose from."

Legal operations, however, serves not just as a driver of transformation, as O'Carroll describes it, but also as a key support function and enabler of other business departments. Akshay Verma experienced this firsthand as former head of legal operations for Meta and current head of legal operations for Coinbase.

Instead of thinking of legal operations as a driver of change, Verma thinks of it as a support function:

"Legal operations is a support function to a support function—the legal department is a support function to the business, and legal operations supports the legal department. On my team, we call ourselves legal's enablement engine. I'm really into alliteration, so I like that one.

"I would define legal operations as the multidisciplinary approach to squeezing as much juice as you possibly can out of the legal department. There are various aspects to doing that. There's the people aspect. There is the process aspect. There is the technology aspect. At least those three things are tools in the toolkit for legal operations professionals to help them squeeze as much juice as possible out of the legal department.

"I think legal operations suffers less from being regarded as a kind of mythical creature than from a lack of awareness in the broader legal industry. Yes, legal operations has arrived, but there's still a significant lack of understanding of the value that legal operations can add. I fight this on a regular basis at Meta. It's a natural aspect, I think, of being in a field that is relatively new on the scene. I have to educate a lot, a lot. And the next part of this answer has nothing to do with lawyers or the legal profession and everything to do with human beings, which is that we are creatures of habit. We are going to keep doing the same things unless we see that it is in our self-interest to change.

"No one's really going to change unless they see the benefit of doing it for themselves. When I try to dispel the—I like your term 'myth'—around legal operations, I find it is an exercise in understanding two things and then incorporating them into the effort that I'm undertaking: (A) what do I need to educate this group, this person, this

decision maker about with respect to the ins and outs of what we should be doing in operations and why we should be doing those things? (B) how well do I know this person or these people? What have they told me? What has this group told me they really care about? What's really going to move the needle for them?

"I'll give you an example that I found somewhat eye-opening. When I first got to what was, at the time, Facebook, one of my remits was to look at our spending on outside counsel and see what we might be doing differently to help control the spending. I'm a big proponent of value-based pricing rather than hourly fees, regardless of the work. I tackled litigation first. That was a six-month odyssey of educating, convincing, advocating, educating, convincing, advocating before we got the program set up. The team there had been doing the same thing for a long time, so they were good lawyers, they got results for the company. Why would they change? Change is risk. No one is really going to change unless they see the benefit of doing it for themselves.

"One of the points that really got the program across the finish line was when I asked, 'How much time do you spend reviewing your hourly invoices on a monthly basis?' And it was a massive number, because these are huge invoices, as you can imagine. And ask anyone who's ever reviewed invoices—it's 30, 40 pages of entries. Are you really going to dig in and try and cut stuff down where you think a lawyer on the outside has spent too much time on something? You're not going to do that. Now imagine value-based pricing where you've pre-negotiated the pricing, and you're matching numbers on a page. It is a minuscule percentage of the current review time. That was a big deal to them. That really mattered. Now it wasn't the crux of what I was offering, but it was that one little *piece of self-interest for these lawyers that really made a difference for them. And I leaned on that, and said, 'Look, this is icing on the cake, but here's what it's going to look like.' And then I had to deliver. That was the easy part.*

"I think those two things—understanding the value of something new and seeing how it serves peoples' self-interest—really go hand in hand. And I don't think this is unique to legal operations, but it's certainly something that I employ because of the nature of legal operations in the legal industry right now. Maybe in 10 years, we'll be having a different conversation."

BEING FIRST TO BE SECOND

However resistant to change lawyers might be, sooner or later the inevitable occurs, and they must deal with it in one way or another.

When I spoke with Susan Hackett of Legal Executive Leadership, I asked her to discuss how lawyers handle having to deal with change. She sees more than one trend:

"Lawyers—let's be honest—often avoid and even despise innovation; they like to do what they know, the way they've always done it, and they want to be recognized as both competent and excellent at whatever they're doing, so they aren't terribly interested in exploring new ideas. They often lack the resilience to try, fail, and try again. So, when it comes to innovation, they don't like to be the first to try things.

"One of my consulting practice mantras is that lawyers like to be first to be second. Although they don't want to lag, they want to see how other lawyers in marquee-status firms or departments have

done with something new—and whether it succeeded—before they'll agree that something is worth trying, never mind doing.

"I tend to focus on preaching change, not innovation, since every one of us knows in our hearts that the way we've (very lucratively!) worked for the past 100 years is not the way we'll be successful working in the next five years, let alone the more distant future.

"They can get on board with the idea that change is inevitable. The trick is to help them figure out how to let go of what they're doing now by offering well-defined and desirable descriptions for what they'll be doing instead. You can't just say 'change' without telling them where they're going or what they're supposed to do instead (as opposed to talking about all the things they're not supposed to do anymore). Change is scary enough without the threat hanging over your head that your reward at the end of the change cycle is the loss of your job."

I thought Hackett would be a good person to ask for a summary of the current state of the practice of law and the place that change has within it. She started with a note borrowed from Jeff Carr:

"Jeff Carr likes to say that alternative fee arrangements are a lot like teenage sex—every teen likes to talk about it, but very few engage in the practice or do it well. I think the same is true in terms of how much real change is going on. Mindfully improved practices are still not the norm for most lawyers' daily work. And for all the talk, executive leaders in law firms and law departments aren't really demanding change. They aren't supporting or rewarding those who lead change initiatives or operational improvements by hiring, promoting, and bonus-compensating them, and they aren't firing or penalizing the pay of those who don't step up. Indeed, most legal

leaders still invest the bulk of their spending and most honorifics in the most expensive, least innovative, most change-resistant lawyers and firms.

"But I think that changed practices, although progressing slowly, are nonetheless gaining a footing, and even accelerating. They are no longer seen as an exception or alternative, but as a series of intriguing and practical solutions that many are considering, and some are adopting. Once you get beyond the outlier stage in almost anything, adoption tends to rise over time.

"The question is, will this slow progress toward better practices be fast enough for clients, or to stay competitive and relevant in the marketplace? It will be interesting to see which kinds of changes just become the norm naturally—as the use of e-mail simply became the norm even though its introduction had been pilloried by horrified lawyers who swore that using it would be the end of privileged communication.

"I assume that some of those normalized-by-time practices might include project management, value-based fee arrangements, more transparent and predictable pricing, standardized metrics and performance evaluation tactics, and the application of data to improve law practice management. I think there are other change practices that may remain 'heavy lifting,' deemed suitable only for the rare adopters, who apply it in the corners of their workload. Thus, I fear that many of us will risk irrelevance in a few years, as more old-school lawyers are replaced by more efficient and effective systems and providers in law companies, for instance.

"We still think that applying data analytics to legal (not practice management) problems is too hard or fraught with dangers. We buy legal technology and half-heartedly train workers, of whom only some will use 20 percent of the tech's capacity to perform a few easy functions, and the rest is just too hard for us to have to use (don't get me started on moving work over to collaboration platforms).

"We can't imagine applying priorities to or eliminating entire tranches of work that don't justify our full-bore attention, because we're addicted to the urgent or what we understand as our current workload, at the expense of important or the emerging gaps or problems we haven't taken the time to identify and address. We'd rather invest ever more in managing litigation than figure out how to avoid it.

"Here's what I think we need to drive this change: General counsel need to stand up and demand what their clients deserve, and not what their legal teams want to give them (which is often defined as a good result because they got a 5 percent discount). They have to drive the complete re-engineering of their own departments' structure and operations before they can truly demand and leverage improved services from outside providers, from law firms to alternative legal services providers. They need to realize that in-house will be lumped into the same pile of irrelevant, overly expensive, or inefficient workers as their similarly trained and practicing outside brethren.

"The fact that law departments are increasingly likely to keep work in-house because that costs less than outside firms doesn't mean that in-house practitioners drive the right work the right way and get the right results. Nor does it mean that there isn't someone else outside the company and their firms who can deliver the client's preferred results better, faster, and cheaper than either their law firms or their in-house team.

"General counsel have got to stop running legal departments as if they were mini- or institutionally specialized law firms. There are lots of law firms out there for clients to hire if that's what they want.

"General counsel need to rethink service delivery at the next level, just as they were doing when I joined the Association of Corporate Counsel and folks started talking about how they might better leverage their teams to drive value they couldn't rely on getting from their outside firms—back in the first rounds of the value movement.

"The next level requires them to deploy data analytics to inform legal and executive decision-making. It requires them to eliminate, not just better manage, corporate failures or disputes. It requires lawyers to provide astute judgment that helps address and solve complicated problems, not just apply their legal acumen to the interpretation of the regulations governing the industry. It requires them to think about how lawyers can help their clients advance the business, not just defend it when it's sued. And they need a department team that can drive those results, not just talk about them at innovation conferences. Only then will they successfully drive the law firm market to put up or get out of the way.

"People do what they're paid to do, in departments and in firms. Until general counsel make it clear what they are paying their teams— inside and out—to do and not to do, nothing will change fast enough to save us from being replaced by other, more effective providers."

Changing processes is more than just changing a process—it is changing how people operate and how they operate. That requires changing incentives and motivations. Changing processes also requires understanding the larger picture of how different parts of a process fit together currently and should fit together in the future. Collaboration, learning from others, making use of better tools, and knowing what they are, are all part of the recipe for effective and lasting change.

Chapter 11

Artificial Intelligence

"AI and legal tech products that incorporate AI will remain in development. The picture of AI in legal technology could look very different in just a few years."

THE LEGAL INDUSTRY IS REPLETE WITH PRODUCTS AND services touting the power of artificial intelligence (AI). The term AI is used liberally, invoked sometimes as a sales tool, sometimes to demonstrate the power of a product, and sometimes as a buzzword with little support. At best, many of these companies are taking liberties with the definition. That is not to say that some legal technology is not deploying thoughtfully designed, elegant, and powerful algorithms (which is what AI currently is). Some legal technology products certainly are. Whether this rises to the level of constituting a true AI—that is, one that can mimic how the human brain operates—is another thing.

Some legal technology entrepreneurs argue that their products refine and improve their functioning over time, making the performance of these legal technology tools more predictable and advanced, and may call this AI. Others hear that and scoff, saying that machine learning is not intelligence, neither natural nor artificial.[18] But AI is with us, and will continue to be, because no matter how it is defined, AI in legal technology is still largely only in its infancy. To illustrate the point, consider autonomous and semiautonomous vehicles for a moment.

Some of the largest, wealthiest, and most technologically advanced companies on the planet—Google, for example, but also Tesla and other car manufacturers—are investing billions of dollars to create AI systems that are capable of operating autonomous vehicles. These companies not only have some of the best software engineers and data scientists in the world, but the problem they're trying to solve comes with unthinkable amounts of data. Vehicles already operate within the confines of the rules of the road (*e.g.,* control systems, such as lane departure warnings and crash warnings), and onboard sensors on any individual vehicle capture millions of data points a day. Multiply that times millions of cars over extended time periods and the data sets almost have too much information to be useful. And yet, even with billions of dollars deployed by the most sophisticated technology companies, with the best programmers operating within a known system and generating a mountain of data, the problem of building a safe autonomous vehicle is still really hard to solve. Human judgment cannot yet be dispensed with.

Now apply that to the practice of law. Contracting has been automated for some time, and it can serve as an example. The few hundred, or few thousand, contracts that any given organization generates a year is nothing when compared with the data sets being used in mature AI systems. The rules are less clearly defined than in engineering and context matters. Certainly, legal technology companies do not have the resources Google has.

---

[18] IBM says that "machine learning is a branch of artificial intelligence and computer science which focuses on the use of data and algorithms to imitate the way that humans learn, gradually improving its accuracy." *See* https://www.ibm.com/cloud/learn/machine-learning#toc-machine-le-K7VszOk6.

IS AI NECESSARY?

One might question whether AI is necessary. Although many legal technology products have moved beyond simple automation, the industry as a whole still hasn't moved far enough that substituting high-speed, high-frequency machine learning for human intelligence is required (or even possible) in many implementations. But even if it is not needed now—and isn't really ready, either—AI and legal tech products that incorporate AI will remain in development. The picture of AI in legal technology could look very different in just a few years.

I first met Bjarne Philip Tellmann when we worked together at Pearson Education. My blog was then in its early stages and Bjarne was instrumental in inspiring me to continue with it. He is a longtime legal leader, former assistant general counsel of Coca-Cola, former general counsel of Pearson Education, and now general counsel of health care company Haleon. He has engaged in several digital transformation projects, including using tools that made use of AI. I spoke with him about AI's current state and its future in the legal space.

> *"So-called AI has the potential to radically change the way we practice law. I don't think we are there quite yet, but we are seeing the stirrings of it, especially in the finance sector, where the tremendous volume supports its use.*
>
> *"For example, J.P. Morgan developed a contract analytics tool used to analyze commercial loan agreements. It has replaced human analysis and the 360,000 hours of human work required to analyze those agreements. That is massively powerful. Within the next 20 years, we will see the massive impact of it as it moves up the food chain. The speed and processing power of the algorithms in use— what's called AI—will increase exponentially, and that cannot do anything but radically transform the practice of law.*

"However, AI can't do everything. At Pearson Education, we did a study with the Oxford Martin School about jobs of the future, and we found that lawyers will be the third most in-demand job between now and 2030. This is because of some skills lawyers possess that machines cannot easily duplicate, such as originality, creativity, and empathy.

"Another thing to keep in mind is that a lot of what lawyers do, broadly speaking, has a big impact on human beings. For example, if you were facing the death penalty, would you want a machine to tell you that? There are limits to what we want from machines and limits to what technology will do in the medium term, that is, the next 20 years. As for the long term—the next 100 years—who knows?"

For a broader perspective on AI and its developing role within the legal space and society at large, I turned to Kenneth Grady, whose diversity and wealth of experience has given him a uniquely balanced perspective on the purpose of and benefits of AI now and in the future.

AI IN LAW AND SOCIETY

Kenneth A. Grady has been a general counsel, law firm partner, law firm subsidiary CEO, legal industry consultant, and adjunct professor and research fellow. Ken focuses on how lawyers, law firms, and law companies can become innovative, efficient, and affordable legal service providers. He sees things from the perspective of clients, but also has the insights of service providers. I asked him what he thought about the role of AI in the ongoing evolution of law practice, and how attorneys might adapt to the rise of AI-driven tools. He responded:

"Right now, I think the best way to think about AI and law is to break it into two categories. The first category covers AI as a tool in the legal industry, and the second covers the impact of AI as a tool on law and society.

"As a tool in law, AI can help us in many ways, and it can hurt us if we misuse it. In that regard, it is similar to understanding how to use current tools, such as online legal databases. As a lawyer, you need to understand the tools available to you, how to use them, and what they can and cannot do. You have to incorporate them into your practice when it makes sense. Lawyers can leverage AI to free the lawyer to do things AI can't do. Lawyers can also use AI to augment what they do. For example, AI can review thousands of documents in a fraction of the time and with higher accuracy than a lawyer—but AI can't interpret the results of that review. Combined, the lawyer plus AI will deliver a higher-quality product, in less time, and at lower cost than either could do alone.

"Outside the legal industry, AI is having a major impact on society. Laws that were written for human agents should be reconsidered, given that humans are being replaced by the complex algorithms that constitute AI tools. There are many circumstances in which AI can do something, but the real question is, should it do that something? In what settings should we regulate AI? How will tort law handle the volume of data AI uses to answer causation questions? How do we test the integrity of algorithms?

"This second area is especially interesting because technologists are driving forward with their own approaches to answering these questions. They are not waiting for lawyers to tag along. Put bluntly, law is slipping away from lawyers to technologists. This is a his-

toric shift and one that has some very deep implications for society and rule of law."

Ron Friedmann is a thought leader in the legal innovation space, with more than 20 years' experience in the legal field. Ron is an expert in law practice management, outsourcing, knowledge management, contract management, e-discovery, legal marketing, and technology for lawyers. I asked his opinion of the use of AI in the practice of law.

"AI likely will increase client value, but it will take more time than the hype in past years suggested. Common use cases today include document review in discovery and due diligence, legal research, and court analytics, and faster, more accurate ways to classify time narratives and matter types.

"In particular, with software providers embedding the powerful algorithms that constitute AI in core document management systems and enterprise search, we can expect AI to deliver actionable information to lawyers in real time."

Intellectual property law might seem to be a natural home for legal technology—at least for those interested in the intersection of law, technology, and society, such as Nelson Rosario.

Nelson Rosario's practice is focused on counseling clients about, particularly, intellectual property strategy. He has worked in a range of areas, including AI, cryptocurrency, blockchain; smart contracts; financial technologies; trading systems; telemedicine; and network and internet communication. Rosario also has served as an adjunct professor at the Chicago-Kent College of Law at the Illinois Institute of Technology. I asked him to talk about blockchain—what it is and why lawyers should care about it.

"A blockchain is an append-only, censorship-resistant, tamper-evident, distributed ledger consisting of transaction data. Now, you can define each one of those words more deeply and, depending on

the particular blockchain, add additional properties. But at its core, any blockchain will very likely have at least those properties.

"The most prominent blockchain on the planet is the ledger of Bitcoin transactions in Bitcoin, followed by the ledger of ether transactions in Ethereum. As my co-professor and I like to emphasize to our law students, blockchain is fundamentally about trust and organizing human behavior. Those two concepts are at the core of what lawyers do."

Blockchain

Indeed, as Nelson notes, blockchain at its core embodies two values that underlie the legal profession. Blockchain is also a fast-growing part of the technological landscape, both outside and in the context of the legal industry and legal technology. But what exactly is it?

Blockchain is the most common form of the so-called distributed ledger technology. A distributed ledger requires a computer network that is peer-to-peer and consensus algorithms so that the ledger is reliably replicated across a number of computer systems.

Blockchain, at its most basic level, is a linked list—but instead of items being linked together, blocks are linked together. Each block represents a certain amount of time, called block time. Within each amount of time, something has happened; let's say there was a transfer of money.

Digital currencies (cryptocurrencies) are one prominent example of a technology based on blockchain. Unlike traditional currencies, they do not rely on a government institution or a bank to maintain them. The first example of a cryptocurrency was Bitcoin, which was first released in 2009. More than 9,000 cryptocurrencies now exist, with a total market capitalization of more than $1 billion.[19]

Other blockchain use cases for the legal industry have been identified by Consensys, a leading software company that makes applications using blockchain. They include smart contracts, chain of custody matters, automated regulatory compliance, machine-to-machine transactions, and, potentially, a blockchain-based arbitration system.

A so-called smart contract is self-executing code—a computer protocol used to electronically facilitate, verify, or enforce an agreement between parties. They are also trackable and irreversible because they are stored on blockchain. The concept is not new; it was first described by Nick Szabo in 1997. Smart contracts allow the exchange of property (or anything of value) without the need for a middleman. Often a smart contract will require that something happen before the contract takes effect, *e.g.*, a payment or certain information being provided.[20]

One prominent example of a smart contract is a decentralized autonomous organization (DAO). A DAO is an organization run through rules that are executed as smart contracts. Because they are still new, their legal status and regulation are still being developed. A DAO represents an application of blockchain and smart contracts to the job of running an organization. A somewhat notorious example of a decentralized autonomous organization was "The DAO," a DAO for venture capital funding. The DAO was launched with $150 million in crowdfunding in June 2016, implementing its smart contracts through Ethereum, and was immediately hacked and drained of $50 million in cryptocurrency.

There are also limited liability autonomous organizations, which are for-profit organizations that are decentralized and enable those who are members of the organization to invest in early-stage Ethereum (an open-source blockchain) projects.

---

[19] Schwab Center for Financial Research. "Cryptocurrencies: What Are They?" June 14, 2022.
[20] For more information on smart contracts and decentralized applications, *see* https://www.gemini.com/cryptopedia/smart-contract-examples-smart-contract-use-cases and www.stateofthedapps.com.

Considering that lawyers spend much of their time on administrative work, using smart contracts could allow the automation of non-billable administrative tasks and transactional work, which could lead to the more efficient delivery of legal services at lower cost. Security remains a huge concern for the legal industry; hackers have grown smarter at accessing secure materials stored by legal departments and law firms. Legal documents can sometimes serve as a honeypot for hackers who try to retrieve sensitive documents for purposes of profit. Rather than e-mailing sensitive data, lawyers can choose to store legal information on a decentralized, secure, and distributed platform where changes can easily be tracked and noticed.

NFTs

In the world of intellectual property, non-fungible tokens (NFTs) have taken hold. An NFT is a cryptographic token that can be used to represent (and secure) a unique property on a blockchain. Using a blockchain, artists or content creators can upload and secure work. When an NFT is transferred via a blockchain, an accurate record of the transfer is created. This builds a clean and transparent chain of custody that can ensure the authenticity of a work. In the art world, assurance of authenticity can result in higher prices for some works of art.

THE FUTURE IS HERE

A further application of blockchain is Web3. Web3 refers to the (still theoretical) next iteration of the internet, a proposed new model where the internet comprises decentralized applications and services built on blockchain and other decentralized technologies, including decentralized exchanges (DEXs), NFTs, and DAOs.

Web3 envisions blockchain technology as its foundation. Web3 advocates propose that using these types of applications will provide an internet environment that is more secure and more transparent than the current world-wide web. They propose that by relying on blockchain, transactions in Web3 are more secure, verifiable, and resistant to tampering. This is groundbreaking in that it reimagines what the internet looks like. In today's world, the internet is centralized where several huge companies control and run large chunks of it and user data is, for many of these companies, far more valuable than gold.

The term Web3 was first coined by Ethereum founder Gavin Wood in 2014.[21] The terms Web 1.0 and Web 2.0 refer to periods of the internet's development as it evolved from message boards and centralized information hubs to what it is today. Specifically, Web 1.0 refers to the period from 1991 to 2004 and Web 2.0 started in 2004 and exists to this day.[22]

A developing phenomenon likely to play a larger role within society, including the legal space, is one facilitated by technology: the metaverse, which is a digital representation of the world. Individuals participate in the metaverse through virtual reality and augmented reality tools. The metaverse is important to consider because of its potential to provide an environment for all, regardless of everyone's physical location. Within it, people can act as they do in the physical world—exchanging ideas, selling and trading services and products, and creating new things. Anyone with an internet connection can, theoretically, participate in it.

Jon Mitchell Jackson, co-founder of ManeuVR and 2013 California Litigation Lawyer of the Year, said it best:

> *"I believe web technologies like blockchain, smart contracts, non-fungible tokens, decentralized finance, decentralized applications, and digital currency will have a more significant effect on the legal profession than the internet. When you add artificial intelligence, virtual reality, and metaverses into the equation, consumer experi-*

---

[21] Gilad Edelman, "The Father of Web3 Wants You to Trust Less," Wired Business, November 29, 2021.
[22] Graham Cormode and Balachander Krishnamurthy, Key Differences Between Web 1.0 and Web 2.0," First Monday, Vol. 13, No. 6, June 2, 2008. https://doi.org/10.5210/fm.v13i6.2125.

ences and expectations will drive new and better ways for lawyers to deliver more efficient, effective, and accurate services.

"One hundred years from now, when we look back on legal history, we'll see that the impact the printing press, pony express, telegraph, telephone, radio, television, fax machine, and internet had on our profession will be miniscule compared to what's about to happen with Web3 and these other technologies. Change is happening in real time right before our eyes. Savvy lawyers are embracing this change, and their vision and actions will define the future practice of law and, in the end, make the world a better place."

Lest you think the metaverse is theoretical or a far-away future state, consider this: Online worlds already exist and attract millions of participants, as did the virtual worlds of Fortnite and Roblox.

J.P. Morgan estimates the future value of the metaverse to be $1 trillion and has taken steps to open a virtual office in Decentraland, a popular metaverse world.[23] Facebook's parent company even changed its name to Meta to reflect a belief in the power of the metaverse.

You may be asking yourself, so if Web3 is the proposed future, *what is the internet of today called?*

A brief history lesson may be in order. The term web is shorthand for the World Wide Web, which is the core of what the internet is today. A computer scientist named Tim Berners-Lee is widely credited with coining the term World Wide Web and with creating the initial World Wide Web.[24]

Web 1.0 refers to what was the first iteration of the World Wide Web where pages were static, mostly text, and users who read these pages didn't contribute content to them. Web 2.0 is what some call the current internet where pages are dynamic, users are often con-

---

[23] Yvonne Lau, "J.P. Morgan Bets Metaverse Is a $1 Trillion Yearly Opportunity As It Becomes First Bank to Open in Virtual World," Fortune, February 1, 2022.
[24] Source: https://webfoundation.org/about/sir-tim-berners-lee/.

tributing content themselves, and the diverse services found online encompass a wide range like social networking sites, blogs, and myriad service vendors. The increase in types of digital devices and their processing power has contributed to the explosive growth of the internet and Web 2.0.

Web 3.0 is the term used to refer to what many are envisioning as the next version of the internet, a decentralized version using blockchain technology.

As for the societal and legal implications of Web 3.0, there are a few major ones worth noting:

- Security and privacy: Users of Web3 will be able to benefit from enhanced security and privacy since the network is decentralized, where there is no sole point of failure prone to exploitation by hackers or other malicious actors. Since blockchain, which relies on distributed ledgers that cannot be retroactively changed unless the original creator provides their consent, underlies Web3, users will have direct and sole control over their data—their data cannot be sold or misused without their consent.

- Financial flexibility: Another implication of Web3 is the ability for there to be greater financial flexibility. With a decentralized network, users could engage in financial transactions without the need for a third party, like a bank or other financial institution, mediating the transaction. A key element of this flexibility is the opportunity for users to engage in decentralized exchanges. Decentralized exchanges, also known as DEXs, allow users to buy and sell digital assets, such as cryptocurrencies, directly with each other, without the need for banks or financial institutions to take part. Users also can use digital currencies like Bitcoin and Ethereum, which also allow for transacting without the support of banks.

- Accountability and transparency: Another important aspect of Web3 is the potential for greater accountability and transparency. Web3 would facilitate this by allowing for secure, transparent, and tamper-proof record-keeping. In a Web3 world, information is stored on a decentralized network of computers rather than just on one server. This means that it is tougher to manipulate data since it is stored across multiple servers. In addition, by using cryptographic algorithms which is what would occur with Web3, any information stored in Web3 would be unable to be changed, making all data and the transfers of such data permanent. These elements of Web3 hold the potential to make it a powerful tool for promoting accountability and transparency online, particularly in industries where trust and transparency are crucial, such as finance and supply chain management.

To learn more about Web3, one can turn to various sources such as relevant courses offered by Udemy and Coursera, blogs such as *DeFi Pulse*, and the website for the Web3 Foundation, which helps fund efforts focused on building Web3.

Chapter 12

The Marketplace
and the Evolving State of Play

"Among those new, better ways to work and think may be a form of collaboration that goes beyond cooperation between departments or between different firms in allied industries."

N OT EVERYONE THINKS THAT THE U.S. LEGAL SYSTEM IS altogether what it should be. The evolving legal landscape includes a number of responses to the problem of limited access from people with a variety of experience.

Mark Deuitch is an entrepreneur and the founder of two web-based start-ups, PeopleClaim (an online dispute resolution service) and RHUbarb (an alternative dispute resolution process that uses online "juries" of industry insiders, legal experts, and public jurors, supported by RHUCoin). Mark is devoted, in his words, to solving "societal issues that are not sufficiently resolved by the existing system." I asked for his thoughts on the legal technology market.

"I'm a recovering investment banker. I used to finance tech companies until I found the tech geek side more interesting than the finance side. Law seemed like a great challenge for technological innovation—so we created an application to try to improve it.

"The problem with law as we saw it was that the legal system has become too expensive and complex to serve its original purpose for smaller claims or less wealthy litigants. There's also an obvious mismatch: the legal system is geared toward adjudication, but most cases are resolved by negotiation. So, we thought that if we could create a negotiation-based process, it could save a lot of people the cost of gearing up for litigation, only to negotiate a settlement after months of expense and acrimony.

"An accessible and inclusive legal system is vital to any democracy—but by some estimates, more than 80 percent of Americans are effectively disenfranchised from civil justice because they cannot afford the time and money costs of going to court. In many cases, they can't even find representation unless their case can become part of a class or be enlarged to suggest a higher potential payout.

"So, by providing an effective alternative for smaller claims in PeopleClaim, we felt we could help free up the courts and lawyers to focus on cases that require actual litigation, while providing a more efficient alternative for the rest."

I asked Larry Bridgesmith to describe the evolution of the legal industry as he understood it. Bridgesmith is an adjunct professor at Vanderbilt University Law School and founder of LegalAlignment, intended to help lawyers better manage their workflows and matters more efficiently. A major change has taken place in lawyer–client relations:

> "Admittedly, a geeky, gadget– and techie-centric personality promotes an interest in legal technology. That part was easy. However, an interest in innovation in law is a direct result of 40 years of legal practice, during which I observed the decreasing trust that clients gave to lawyers and the rocket ride attorneys enjoyed to the top of the economic ladder.

> "In the decade before 2010, the cost of living increased 25 percent (2.5 percent per year on average). During the same period, lawyers' compensation increased 75 percent. Driven by the billable hour, the traditional business model has proven to be a perverse incentive that rewards inefficiency and worse. Billing practices drove a business model based on cost-plus pricing, which protected the law firm at the expense (literally) of the client. Selling input (time) is far more lucrative than selling output (value).

> "Lawyer–client relations are now radically different than they were in 1978. The corporate clients I served over that time are more sophisticated because they are competing in a global economy that applies management methodologies, such as Six Sigma and Lean to the 'better, faster, cheaper' mantra required to survive. Those are the clients that are impacting the business model of law today.

> "The Consortium of Legal Operations Counsel and the Association of Corporate Counsel are moving into the driver's seat. In-house counsel are mobilizing and combining resources to instruct outside counsel how legal services will require legal project management, mandatory billing guidelines, fixed fees, and transparency. The

Georgetown Law and Thomson Reuters Legal Executive Institute's "2018 Report on the State of the Legal Market" reveals that the legal market for high-end legal services is shrinking.

"At the same time, Big Law is doubling down on a failing strategy. Alternative legal law models, from legal process outsourcers and managed legal service providers to the growth of in-house legal departments and Big Four accounting firms, are all invading the province of Big Law to meet client needs and expectation. The Legal Executive Institute report calculates that $10 billion in revenues previously paid to Big Law has been captured by these alternative legal services providers. Corporate procurement officers and reverse auctions are increasingly taking the place of country club friendships and good-old-boy networks as criteria for choosing outside counsel.

"Mark Harris, former CEO of Axiom Managed Solutions, maintains that 200 companies purchase 80 percent of legal services provided. That is awesome buying power. At the other end of the legal market, numerous studies and anecdotal evidence support the astonishing reality that 80 percent of potential legal clients in the United States (both individuals and businesses) 'go it alone' when confronted with a need for legal representation.

"The reasons for not using lawyers to address legal concerns are many. The lack of affordable, accessible, and approachable lawyers is among them. If 90 percent of lawyers aspire to serve 200 clients at 'bet the company' prices, the math doesn't work. The competition is fierce.

"The mass consumer market is left in the lurch. Serving the 80 percent that are currently not served will require legal services that are, literally, better, faster, and cheaper. Billable-hour pricing and

traditional legal business models will not bridge the gap. If 100 percent of the legal market could be served with prices that clients are willing and able to pay, there would not be enough lawyers to meet the need. Only massive innovation in legal service delivery can meet these systemic needs. Legal technology is a set of tools that can assist."

Mark Deuitch and Larry Bridgesmith are far from alone in seeing that the traditional legal services system is no longer working well for far too many people; recall Documate's Dorna Moini and legal business consultant Mark A. Cohen.

Cohen is the CEO of Legal Mosaic, a legal business consultancy that provides strategic advice to corporate legal departments, law firms, legal service providers, legal networks, entrepreneurs, and law schools. He is also a co-founder and executive chairman of the Digital Legal Exchange, a global not-for-profit organization "committed to accelerating digital transformation."[25]

Cohen has seen the legal marketplace from all sides—as a provider, manager, and consumer of legal services. He has spent decades "trying to improve legal delivery—first as a lawyer, later as an outside general counsel and receiver, and finally as an entrepreneur," Cohen notes. "Technology is one of three pillars that support delivery of legal services; the other two are legal and business expertise. Technology is as much an element of legal delivery as differentiated practice skills and judgment, and it's more pervasive."

Cohen has also thought about adopting an approach to law firm ownership and structure that is more like that of the United Kingdom, where there is somewhat greater flexibility regarding the delivery of legal services, as "long overdue," Cohen adds. "But I confess to having 'alternative business structure envy.' How can re-regulation be resisted when about 85 percent of Americans lack access to legal services, and tools exist to ameliorate that deplorable situation? The

---

[25] https://www.dlex.org/.

regulators [such as the American Bar Association and individual state bar organizations] should focus on the public, not on the lawyers."

For Ron Friedmann, who has three decades of experience in the legal market, the most surprising development that he has seen is "that so many in the legal market talk about innovation. Why is that a surprise?" He went on to say:

"I have three decades of legal market experience inside two law firms, two legal software companies, two consulting firms, and a legal process outsourcing company. I have seen, and led, change and innovation many times. For example, in 1990, I worked on substantive legal hypertext systems. That was pre-Web, and it took 30-plus minutes just to explain the hypertext concept!

"Each decade has seen big technology and legal business changes, yet not spawned constant talk of innovation. The 1990s saw personal computers on lawyers' desks, the internet used for commercial purposes, and the beginning of e-discovery. Law firm affiliates were also big. The 2000s saw mobile devices, the beginning of social media, and the start of cloud-based applications. Alternative legal service providers began to appear. The 2010s saw the swift spread of mobile apps, vast social media penetration, and the rapid rise of cloud computing. Law firms changed their leverage model, with many firms adding lower-cost delivery models.

"That's a lot of change and innovation, but it did not cause innovation buzz. I suggest three reasons for that buzz now. First, clients have recognized their buying power and demand value. They bring work in-house or use alternative providers. That puts pressure on firms to practice more efficiently—and clients treat innovation as a proxy for value. Second, we all experience disruption daily: the rise of self-service, the decline of retailers, the rise of sharing services

such as Uber and Airbnb, and the rapid advances in self-driving cars. Everyone expects big changes, and fast. And third, the rise of artificial intelligence, both in the market at large and in the legal industry, has spawned hope, fear, and a slew of legal start-ups. It also has gotten many lawyers focused on innovation more broadly."

LOOKING FOR TRANSFORMATION

Jack Newton's identification of cloud computing as transformative, Susan Hackett's distinction between sustaining and transformative change, as well as the experience of daily disruptions in many areas of life—let alone in law—are among the things that speak to what is perhaps an understated search for transformative change.

Long-time legal tech innovator Maya Markovich, who is currently executive in residence at Village Capital and executive director at the Justice Technology Association, has a necessary passion for transforming the practice of law. She is currently focused on building momentum for innovation within the ecosystem of Dentons, the largest multinational law firm in the world. I sat down with her to discuss modernization and the business of law, asking, first, how she would define modernizing the legal profession. Her reply touched on some common themes:

"The legal profession is feeling a broad urgency to rise to modern standards, leveraging current tools, available data, and processes. Since the law hasn't really benefited from these advances as other industries have, lawyers can look at modernization as leveraging the lessons others have learned about operating in a global economy, with all the constraints and benefits of today's world. Clients are often more advanced in this area, pushing their lawyers' firms to eliminate outdated processes and adopt the standards of flexibility, efficiency, and transparency that clients are already using.

"Innovation—constantly trying new things, consciously avoiding preconceived notions or biases, and thinking expansively and creatively about ways to solve problems—is a much more difficult, messier mandate than modernization. But it's necessary to focus on applying new methods to existing workflows and adapting existing workflows to new demands. For substantive progress toward growth, improved efficiency, and increased access to justice, we have to make this tectonic shift as an industry. Law has been essentially static for generations, and we must be looking for opportunities to find new, better ways to work and think."

Among those new, better ways to work and think may be a form of collaboration that goes beyond cooperation between departments or between different firms in allied industries. Quddus Pourshafie, for one, looks forward to collaboration on a larger scale. He has dedicated himself to moving the needle in the legal industry through FutureLab.Legal, a rare institution that bridges the gaps between stakeholders in the legal industry to generate solutions. His interest in legal innovation started early:

"Coming out of law school, I was abruptly presented with the reality of the inner workings of law firms and the legal industry. The standard assumptions about the business of law and 'the path to partnership' expectations, along with a general apathy and a lack of curiosity on those I spoke with, including my peers, led me to try to understand this system I was becoming a part of.

"This took a year or so, and then there were many questions that were left unchallenged or answered with 'it's always been like this.' Other cultural truths or traditions were not really explained but were certainly felt—for example, customs concerning gender imbalance, power dynamics, seniority complexes, and elitist inner circles that were often predominantly of a single race. However, because I

was driven by curiosity and a passion that things could be better, I found there were also many great things happening or about to happen in this industry, as tradition started to give way to new ways of approaching the work of law.

"I also found that, whenever a group of stakeholders would gather from different pillars of the legal industry (I've split them into legal services providers/market, institutions/universities, regulators/government, and legal technology), they would handball a lot of the issues to one another, each waiting for the other to make a move. Within those interactions and the many conversations I had with the different stakeholders, I found gaps. This is where Future-Lab.Legal became a concept: a place where all stakeholders can come to find solutions and pivot into the future of law.

"This broad vision gave me the necessary agility to be part of many conversations and to become useful to many projects, all of which continue to give me insight into where things may be going."

While technology continues to advance rapidly in so many areas of society, resistance to technology within the legal space remains formidable, driven in large part by fear. However, clients are not hesitant to learn more about how technology can help them stand out on the business front and are starting to demand more from those they turn to for legal support and guidance. "To remain competitive, we need to increase productivity while enhancing the quality of legal processes against an ever-decreasing cost base. To achieve this, there is no other solution than to embrace technology," notes Johan Huizing, associate general counsel for Europe, the Middle East, and Africa at Itron.[26]

Gartner, a leading research firm, predicts the following for the future of the legal technology space and legal departments: Legal de-

---

[26] "The State of Play," *GC* magazine.

partments will increase their spending on legal technology fivefold by 2025; and even earlier, by 2024, legal departments will have replaced 20 percent of their generalist lawyers with non-lawyer specialists.[27]

On the law firm side, firms that want to retain and enlarge their client base will continue to meet their clients where they are, enabled by technological solutions and driven by data and analytics. Yet, for all of technology's effects, if I were to make one prediction about the future of the legal tech space, it would be this: technology will not be the key driver of innovation and change within the law—people and culture will. The more legal culture embraces technology, the more change will happen.

---

[27] Rob Van Der Meulen, "Five Legal Technology Trends Changing In-House Legal Departments," Insights, Legal and Compliance, February 24, 2022.

Chapter 13

Dealing with Change

"Perhaps a larger change is needed—a change to a widespread culture of innovation. That term, though, can mean different things to different people."

PETER DRUCKER IS KNOWN FOR SAYING THAT CULTURE eats strategy for breakfast. In the legal space, this couldn't be truer. The biggest area of resistance to technology within the legal world appears to be an inherent cultural fear of technology driven by financial incentives not to change. The billable-hour model, which rewards inefficiency and a lack of desire to do things differently from how they have always been done, is among these incentives. There are others.

Consider, for example, how much time is spent in law schools focusing on the history of the law and of laws and how little time is spent on the practical elements of the practice of law and the delivery of legal services. When one enters the legal workforce so steeped in history and how things have always been done, it is challenging, to say the least, to consider doing things another way.

RESISTING CHANGE

Dealing with change may require more than overcoming lawyers' resistance to new procedures or tools—although that may still be required, too. Marlene Gebauer, global director of strategic legal insights at Greenberg Traurig, LLP, and host of the popular *The Geek in Review* podcast, has dealt with such resistance, and she has some suggestions that others might use:

"You must be aware of where the opportunities are and likely will be. Look at the landscape of possible solutions, and target your efforts. Not everyone is interested in innovation, and unless they are pressed, they won't be. Send the message of innovation broadly, but focus on the people and groups who are receptive and have a scalable use in mind. Build on that vertically in those groups, and scale the effort to other groups. For example, we built a couple of internal models for analytics that can be used more broadly for various kinds of data and by different departments.

"And don't forget to stay creative regarding potential new opportunities. Clients' needs are changing rapidly, so keeping current via internal firm communication and news sources is important.

"It is also a good idea, if your organization is very resistant to change or if you just need to take a first step, to focus on a small change and build on that. For example, we introduced technology that does what lawyers already do, but faster and more accurately. This isn't a big step to take for most, because they see it as the help

that it is. Once users are comfortable with that, you can perhaps begin to introduce technology that changes the work process.

"I would be remiss not to say, ... that there is an opportunity to introduce and welcome more users to innovative solutions. Given the need for social distancing, there is a need even for those who are resistant to get on board with the technology and processes that are available. How they experience that—good or bad—is in our hands, so let's make it good. That way there is a better chance they will accept change for the long term."

Part of my conversation with Susan Hackett focused on how lawyers handle having to deal with change. She spoke of more than one challenge:

"I see two concurrent types of change taking place in the profession: sustaining change and transformational change. Sustaining change is important but not revolutionary; it's automating or improving the efficiency or output of what you've always done as a lawyer. Sustaining change allows you to continue to perform the same work you've always done, but better, faster, or cheaper.

"Transformational change is much harder and more aggressive; it involves practices that force you out of the roles you know and the work you've always done to do something else entirely. When the entire IP team moves from portfolio management to a managed service provider that uses trained employees, technology, and automation to handle the operational IP needs of the company, and those lawyers are then embedded in the company's product development group, where they think about new ways to push forward ideas and inventions that will allow the company to lead the market, that's transformational change.

"Transformational change allows legal departments to push contract formation and daily contract management back to clients through a do-it-yourself contract system; there is no role for a whole team of in-house contract lawyers anymore (just a few to handle outlier deals and manage the system), so the question is what will those lawyers do instead? Where will they go? Transformational change requires lawyers and legal teams to understand how to do less law (at least as we are used to defining it) and do more leading. It aligns them with roles and work product that help advance the company's business or that anticipate problems and avoid them, rather than roles that focus on responding remedially if and when trouble arises."

While the legal industry continues to evolve, the question arises of how to establish a widespread culture of innovation within a field that has been built on long-standing traditions. Perhaps a larger change is needed—a change to a widespread culture of innovation. That term, though, can mean different things to different people. I asked Varun Mehta, CEO of Factor, what he thought. He shifted the question a little:

"To begin with, let's accept that 'innovation' is becoming an overused word that can mean any number of different things to different people.

"My take on innovation is that it's whatever it takes to turn ideas into solutions that actually deliver value and advantage to customers. It's about changing the nature of work and the outcome achieved. It's not about just tech apps, tools, or features in isolation.

"I've been in this space for a while now, and I've never felt more energized about the momentum and recognition for the need to inno-

vate in the legal market now. So, how do we continue to build and spread this culture?

"Be rooted in the customer value proposition. What matters most are things perhaps customers aren't even aware of.

"We have to be prepared to try things. They may not always work, but we have to start somewhere and refine as we go."

LOOKING BACK

"We have to start somewhere"—true enough. Generally, you start from where you are, which reflects where you have been. I couldn't resist asking Jack Newton, Clio's founder, about his thoughts on how the legal profession had progressed from when he started, and on where it might go over the next four or five years. He had quite a few things to say:

"I think it's been a very steady progression of transformation over the decade-plus I've been in the legal industry. I've seen, with the firms we work with, a real appetite for technology, especially an appetite for technology that really affects the client experience. Even the way we view the services we're delivering at Clio has evolved from focusing on raw productivity enhancements—thinking about the back office of the law firm and how do you do things slightly faster, slightly more efficiently and more competently, maybe with less risk—to looking at that as almost a table stake in terms of what technology can deliver.

"So now, we can start thinking about how to fundamentally trans-form everything about the way we deliver legal services, thanks to technology, and how we can do a ground-up reimagining of the way consumers get connected with lawyers, the way they see their legal

services delivered to them, and the way they build ongoing relationships with lawyers.

"It's been very exciting to see the progress we've been able to make over the past decade in helping drive the adoption of technologies that enable that transformation. We've seen, I think, a decade-plus of progress in just six months, during the pandemic, in terms of accelerating that technology adoption cycle, accelerating some of the transformation that was already underway. Many lawyers are waking up to the fact that the cloud is not a nice-to-have for some more forward-looking law firms to deploy—it is instrumental and foundational to the way lawyers need to deliver legal services to their clients, now and in the future.

"We've helped pivot legal service delivery amid COVID-19, not just to a new normal, but to a better normal, where we've got better adoption of technology and reduced emphasis on one of the huge pieces of overhead for law firms, which is physical offices, expensive offices, and premier office space in downtown locales. This has shifted to what we've discovered many clients actually prefer, which is legal services delivered over a Zoom call or delivered over the Internet, supported by best-in-class technology to make that process more efficient.

"Regarding technology adoption, I think we're seeing something that would have played out over a decade but has been compressed into a much smaller timeframe, where the law firms that are embracing technology are pulling ahead and becoming the rightful winners of the market in the COVID-19 landscape. They are rapidly outpacing law firms that are maybe stuck in their old ways. I think, before COVID-19, those law firms probably could've coasted for an-

other decade and done okay. And I think those are the law firms that will soon start to struggle in a really profound way, if they're not already. They're going to see a market consumed by the innovative law firms in the marketplace, firms that are meeting consumers where consumers want to be."

Looking back over a shorter range, of the past five years or so, Catherine Krow of Digitory Legal had this to say:

"Law firms are experiencing big changes in the way clients expect them to deliver services. We are slowly starting to see these demands filter down to individual lawyers, and this trend will continue. In the past, lawyers have been very skeptical about change management, particularly about adopting new processes and technology. But clients will no longer tolerate this resistance to change.

"Being a lawyer now demands more than just writing the perfect brief. It used to be you could put your head down, work hard, and you would succeed. But now you need to take a more holistic view of your clients' needs.

"And there are structural and regulatory constraints within law firms and the legal system that have to be overcome before we will see a fundamental shift in the way law firms operate. But some firms out there are making fundamental changes in the way they operate, and professional conduct rules are changing, so there is hope. I believe there is enough momentum to solve these systemic problems, as clients will no longer accept lawyers' special snowflake status."

Olga V. Mack, founder of the legal tech company Parley Pro (now part of LexisNexis) thinks that lawyers today, especially relatively new lawyers, should be prepared for near-constant change. She includes corporate counsel in this, saying:

> *"The way you practice law will change at least seven to ten times in your legal career. An open mind, curiosity, and an attitude of lifetime learning will be your biggest assets and competitive advantage.*
>
> *"For example, as COVID-19 spread around the world, it was often up to a company's office of general counsel to help that company be ready, stay nimble, and continue to thrive during the epidemic.*
>
> *"This crisis highlights the increasingly critical role and effect of corporate counsel in the modern world. Counsel's ability to solve new problems and lead under pressure are key even though law school likely did not prepare them for this type of global crisis."*

FACING REALITY

If the practice and profession of law are in upheaval, those who are now in the legal industry will have to make some adjustments— or go into another line of work. That sums up what can be a quite difficult process of change. I spoke with some leading industry analysts about how risk-averse lawyers can adjust and what barriers to change they might encounter. According to Jordan Furlong, the first step is to face reality:

> *"Lawyers are certainly risk averse—and failure averse and embarrassment averse, too. But everyone is change-averse when they've got a status quo worth protecting, and that's where the legal profession is right now—hanging on tightly to a system that lawyers understand and that works to their overall benefit.*

"I can sympathize, to a certain extent, with lawyers who are being forcibly evicted from their comfort zone by all the changes in the market. I know it's hard. But at a certain point, all our aversions become an excuse for not acting, and I don't have much sympathy for that. The facts are what they are, and they've been clear to anyone who's cared to look for the past 10 years. Willful blindness is not a strategy.

"The way to start adjusting is to start facing reality. Regardless of whether the good old days were ever all that good, we have a new set of circumstances now: legal services buyers with more knowledge, more options, and more confidence than they've ever had, up against law firms whose 19th-century business models aren't responding the way they used to. I wish more law firms would recognize and accept that we're not going back to the way things were. Clients aren't going to become dumber and meeker. Technology is not going to stop doing work that only lawyers were once able to do. The law firms and in-house teams that are ahead of the game now aren't necessarily any smarter or better than anyone else. What sets them apart is that they saw change underway, they accepted it, and they dealt with it. Denial puts you at a competitive disadvantage.

"I probably over-rely on this quote, but I think Samuel Johnson's observation, 'When a man knows he is to be hanged in a fortnight, it concentrates the mind wonderfully,' has some relevance here. You might not like swimming, but if the boat you're on is burning as it sinks below the waterline, you can probably reconcile yourself to jumping in."

Facing the reality of the current marketplace doesn't mean only adjusting to changes in software. The law firms' "19th-century business models" that aren't responding the way they used to are not the only traditional models of legal practice that are being challenged. Every in-house law department these days is trying to figure out how to balance a heavier workload with dwindling resources.

Bjarne Tellmann, general counsel of the health solutions company, Haleon, thinks this is the heart of the disruption of the legal profession:

> *"If you think about the ongoing disruption of the profession, at the heart of it you have the more-for-less challenge. It is a bit ironic in that usually a surge in demand means an increase in supply—but within the legal field, it's just the opposite.*

> *"The reason why can be tied to three big causes. First, there has been an explosion in regulatory growth. Legislative rules have increased, and each rule has been accompanied by increases in penalties. Second, our world, and the rules governing it, have become increasingly complex, as have the issues arising from the rules. More, those issues tend to flow freely across borders and across jurisdictions. Third, there is what I call risk convergence. Legal risks are now much more than just legal risks; they can also be reputational risks, human resources (personnel) risks, financial risks, and so on. They can take on lots of different dimensions and travel at the speed of Twitter.*

> *"There is also the fact that companies have faced increased pressure on their bottom lines. In many cases, there has been a decline in a company's profit. Accompanying this decline in profit has been a decline in resources.*

"You address this problem through tools and processes that have emerged in the face of these numerous forces and pressures. Technology has been a large driver of these new tools and processes. Broadly speaking, this means that the one-stop-shop of law firm solution is no longer the only game in town. The value chain is coming undone, and general counsel are now able to unbundle and package pieces of the value chain to other providers, e.g., outsourcing, near-shoring solutions to staffing, and the rise of the 'super-temp,' who does substantive work on a contract basis. Some law firms subcontract some of their work to smaller firms.

"As for technology, there are the basics, e.g., e-mail tools and videoconferencing. There is also now a vast array of self-help tools, such as tools that allow you to pull templates off the cloud for standard form agreements you previously had to go to a firm for. Moreover, there are now contract management systems that allow for more efficient administration of contract processes, e-billing systems, and so on, not to mention AI and machine-learning applications.

"The rise of these new tools requires our people to be trained in new skills and possess new abilities. That is the challenge for the next decade: producing a workforce for today's world. At the same time, this has required our people to have new skills and new abilities. One piece of this, I think, is having law schools bring more business school courses into the curriculum, such as finance, leadership, even marketing."

TEACHING A NEW WAY

Several people I spoke with thought that changing the curriculum at many law schools would go far toward graduating lawyers who are more prepared to practice than today's graduates. Jordan Furlong, for one, suggests that law schools be given:

> *"a new standard of achievement for their graduates to meet, and refuse to admit to practice any graduate who doesn't meet it. Many law schools will shut down, unable to adjust to that new standard. Many others will adjust and start producing lawyers who can provide value upon graduation."*

Once the newly minted juris doctor leaves the law library, Jordan Furlong has more advice:

> *"Becoming a really good lawyer takes years of training, mentoring, and experience. We talk about law schools producing 'practice-ready lawyers,' and that's fine as far as it goes, but let's be clear: that means 'lawyers who are minimally competent to provide value to clients,' not 'lawyers who are at the top of their game on day one.'*
>
> *"It's important that new lawyers understand there is a lot for them to learn, and it's going to take them most of their careers to do it.*
>
> *"The first rule is to be patient with yourself as you learn. The second rule is to find someone to work for who will be equally patient with you, but who will also be demanding. And know that over the course of your career, regardless of what sector of the market you're in, you'll need to display certain skills consistently. The earlier you can get trained in their use and experienced in their application, the better. My top three are:*

> 1. *Negotiation: The ability to negotiate is absolutely essential, and far more important, to my mind, than advocacy, which is becoming a niche area. Every interaction with a client, a colleague, or opposing counsel will require negotiation skills to advance your own interests while remaining aware*

and respectful of the other side's interests (which does not mean advancing their own interests equally with yours).

2. *Empathy: Some people are naturally empathetic; the rest of us have to work at it. Place yourself in the other person's position. See the world through their eyes. Listen actively to what they tell you, and show that you've heard them. It's not only essential to client service and negotiation, but also to staying in touch with your own humanity, which many years in the law can slowly alienate you from.*

3. *Collaboration: We've been training lawyers to be lone wolves forever. Grade higher than your law school class-mates, defeat your moot court opponents, compete against your fellow associates, and accumulate individual accom-plishments in billing and origination. Enough of that. In-stead, work with others to advance the team's goals. Be more than the sum of your parts. That's what winning looks like now."*

Furlong and I also talked briefly about his interest in forecasting the future of the legal market. I asked if he agreed with Richard Suss-kind, who emphasizes the increasing importance and value of di-verse legal service models and using technology to create efficiency gains in the practice of law. He replied:

"Forecasting the future was never my interest and isn't really what I do; analyzing the present and advising what to do right now is more my thing. If I see a car speeding toward the edge of a cliff, I don't think I'm forecasting the future if I tell the driver that swerv-ing immediately would be highly advisable.

"I wouldn't be able to do what I do if Richard had not done it first, and better. He's absolutely right about new models and new technology creating efficiency gains and new ways of delivering legal services. But Richard's specialty is technology, and that's the primary lens through which he actually does forecast the future. I'm not remotely a technology expert, so I tend to approach the issue from what I know, the perspective of market dynamics: competition, innovation, profit margins, scalability, and so on. Other people use a different and equally accurate lens.

"The legal market is an intensely complex and multidimensional beast, and the more people we have studying it and making sense of it, the better."

Jordan Furlong wasn't the only expert I asked about making law graduates ready to practice; I also asked Mark Cohen about what advice he would give an attorney who wants to be "practice ready," and what law schools can do better to prepare their graduates for today's legal world. Cohen spoke to both new lawyers and those who had been in practice for a few years:

"'Practice ready' implies new lawyers. If I had my way, law school would be two years, and one-third of that would focus on business training, analytics, and technology. In my view, it's a big waste of societal resources and students' money to spend three years primarily on substantive law, much of which most graduates will never use in practice. Fortunately, some top– and mid-tier law schools are inching toward a more multidisciplinary curriculum. But accreditation rules are a huge barrier to the major educational changes the market needs.

"Back to lawyers with several years or more of practice experience: with a modern definition of 'practice ready'—which might include

being comfortable with technology and analytics—how many are ready? Lawyers at all levels of experience who want to continue delivering value to clients must remain open to new ways of working and to additional training throughout their careers. I would say, if asked, 'know your craft, learn new skills that the marketplace demands (business fluency, collaboration, project management, personal branding, etc.), follow what's happening in the marketplace, be alert to opportunity, be a self-advocate, and meld your passions and pre-law life with your professional one.'"

Richard Tromans has been a longtime legal tech observer, commentator, and analyst, and is the founder and editor of the popular legal technology website *Artificial Lawyer*. I asked him the question I had asked Mark Cohen about practice-ready attorneys. Given his long journey in the legal tech space, I wanted to engage with him in a discussion regarding the resistance to change and to technology, how do we prepare "practice-ready attorneys"? His response was telling.

"This is a very popular question! The answer is to know what's out there. Lawyers can't hope to help a client by leveraging legal technology if they don't understand what can be done. They also need to think about legal data, processes, and linking technologies together. Understanding a bit of code and statistics would be great too, but this is never going to become a core issue for most lawyers. The key is learning how to use data and technology; you don't have to be a coder to use an AI system. But to create a new service line or product through technology tech, you do need to understand what the tools can do.

"I return to the double question: what problems do I want to solve, and what can technology now do for me and my clients? This is the way to go."

If technology is to become a more indelible part of the practice of law, the focus should be *not* on technology itself, but on the outcomes lawyers are seeking to achieve and the tools that will help them achieve those outcomes. The way to find answers to the questions of outcomes and tools should be driven by the needs of those the lawyer is seeking to support and by how that lawyer can be of best value to the business or law firm, and those the lawyer supports within that environment.

One thing is for certain: People will lead the way for change. Technology is there to support and facilitate that change.

Epilogue

*"[L]awyers are being asked to learn new skills and to
think in new ways. A lawyer who fails at this
will be vulnerable to becoming obsolete and
poorly positioned to provide the level of service
expected by today's clients."*

THIS BOOK IS BUT A BRIEF FORAY INTO THE WORLD OF legal technology and innovation. Resources on the subject abound; instead of trying to learn it all, focus on the topics that are most pertinent to what you are trying to achieve.

Learning the concepts and ideas underlying technological tools is important. Learning specific tools just to learn about legal technology tools is less important. And there are some key lessons.

The first lesson is that legal technology and legal innovation can both come in a variety of forms. The second is that legal technology is not required to engage in legal innovation.

Legal technology indeed has led to innovation in the practice of law. However, many innovations have occurred without the use of legal technology, such as the application of Lean and Six Sigma principles within the practice of law. These principles look at existing processes and procedures and seek to improve them and eliminate waste and inefficiencies. The beauty of these principles is that they are scalable. Legal technology may generate the headlines, but innovations that do not rely on technology can have as much of an effect as those that do.

The third lesson is that legal technology is not out to get you or your job. Embrace automation. Technology can automate parts of what a lawyer typically does, especially those tasks that are repeatable, simple, and routine. Automation can allow lawyers to focus on more important and higher-risk work. Lawyers can determine which tasks to automate by looking at existing processes, examining each step of each process, and deciding which ones are routine and repeatable—then go looking for a legal tech product that can perform that routine, repeatable task. Technology now can assist lawyers in the review, analysis, and drafting of legal documents, although not without direction. Much legal technology still requires human judgment to succeed.

And although legal technology may not be about to replace lawyers, legal technology is changing the meaning of what it means to practice law. It also is prompting a rethinking of the skills required to practice law well. This means that lawyers are being asked to learn new skills and to think in new ways. A lawyer who fails at this will be vulnerable to becoming obsolete and poorly positioned to provide the level of service expected by today's clients.

The fourth lesson is that lawyers are already using legal technology. However, they are likely not to be using its full functionality. You are probably using tools such as Slack, Skype, and Microsoft Office. These tools are legal technology in this sense: you write with them, communicate with them, and analyze documents and data with them. These are powerful applications. They offer a plethora of functions, and many of those functions can help you work more effectively and produce better results for your clients. Procertas's online learning software can help you to assess your current level of knowledge of these tools and help you learn how to use them better.[28]

Why should you learn how to use more functions of these products? Learning more will allow you to increase your own productivity by automating some repetitive or time-consuming tasks. By learning how to use the tools you have better, you are improving your level of technological competence, helping to comply with this requirement if it applies in your state, and becoming a more effective lawyer for the 21st century.

The fifth lesson is that collaboration is crucial to the ongoing success of the legal profession. Do not discount its power. At its core, collaboration involves teamwork, engaging others across disciplines and functions and learning. As Heidi K. Gardner, a renowned expert on the topic, notes:

> *"Data shows, when lawyers do work across specialties, their firms earn higher margins, clients are more loyal, and individual lawyers are able to charge more for the work that they do."*[29]

This is hard for those within the legal profession because, historically, lawyers have been taught and encouraged to believe that only they know how to practice law, only they understand the requirements to practice law, and only they recognize a good outcome. This is changing. Not only are the skills needed to practice law increasing and changing, but so are what it means to practice law and what it means to deliver a good outcome.

There is a long-overdue movement to listen more to clients and to provide solutions that are just as much a business solution as a legal solution. The way to deliver business-focused outcomes is to learn

---

[28] See www.procertas.com/.
[29] Heidi K. Gardner, "Collaboration in Law Firms: The New Wave of Client Service," *The Practice*, Center on the Legal Profession, Harvard Law School, Vol. 1, No. 6, September–October 2015.

from those who are close to the business, to incorporate their feedback, and to make use of their skills and expertise. Lawyers do not know it all. Lawyers will never know it all. Lawyers need to accept these facts and take them to heart.

The sixth lesson is that change is hard. Legal technology is introducing new ways to perform legal tasks and deliver legal services. Yet resistance to adjusting to these new ways remains strong. Humans are inherently resistant to change, and the legal profession is especially so. However, lawyers can and do facilitate the reworking of methods, of models, and of work practices by focusing on the people they work with and the work culture.

If you are trying to persuade people to change how they practice law, you need to meet them where they are. This means asking for their input, understanding their needs and concerns, and addressing those needs and concerns. Taking the time to do this will help facilitate a work culture that supports its people and supports change. If people are not ready to use a particular legal technology or not prepared to engage with it, then whatever legal technology tool you choose to deploy will likely be underused, if used at all, and not as effective as it is meant to be.

As Richard Tromans notes, "Culture is expressed through leadership."[30] To enable change within an organization requires that there be support from both inside the team and from leadership. Leaders set the tone for their organizations and employees typically adhere to the tone and style set from the top of the team. But blindly applying a legal technology tool to an existing process without first considering how that existing process works may not improve the process. Just the opposite may occur instead.[31]

This lesson is perhaps no more evident than in the rapid proliferation of legal technology companies. The fact that these companies exist at all is evidence of the changes brought about by technology. The immediate and important work to be done right now is to enable

---

[30] *See* "Culture Eats Legal Tech for Breakfast," *Artificial Lawyer*, May 18, 2020.
[31] For a personal account of these two tasks, read this excellent account of one person's journey, in which Jason Barnwell explains his innovation story: www.legalevolution.org/2019/01/bricklayers-architects-080/.

both people and work cultures to be supportive of this transformation. It is the culmination of these legal technology companies, new business models, and changes in people and processes that will have the most lasting impacts on the profession.

Afterword

"Technology can't just 'happen' to lawyers—lawyers need to engage, if not embrace, the realm of the possible opened up by technology."

B Y NOW, THE TERM "ECOSYSTEM" SHOULD CARRY A deeper meaning, especially when one is reminded of its meaning in the broader business context, according to Investopedia:

> *A business ecosystem is the network of organizations—including suppliers, customers, competitors, government agencies, and so on—involved in the delivery of a specific product or service through both competition and cooperation. The idea is that each entity in the ecosystem affects and is affected by the others, creating a constantly*

evolving relationship in which each entity must be flexible and adaptable to survive as in a biological ecosystem.

The fact that all entities are related and evolve as the result of the actions of others can be either beneficial or detrimental, depending on each members' behaviours.

And I want to see the half-full glass. So, of course, the unarticulated benefit of an ecosystem as defined above is that through relationships and collaboration, each entity individually becomes a bit better; and all of them, through super-additivity, become even more relevant for the ecosystem. A clear case of the whole is greater than the sum of its parts.

It also makes it apparent that you cannot have only one category of entities, say in our case, law firms, but really a broad representation of all players to develop a sustainable ecosystem where all benefit.

Technology has been for a long time an underrepresented member of this ecosystem. That said, whilst its emergence has happened at a glacial pace, the movement has comparatively, massively accelerated in the last couple of decades and even more so in the last couple of months!

For the ecosystem to evolve and survive in a balanced way, technology needs to find its place. As with any relationship, this must be a two-way street: Technology can't just "happen" to lawyers—lawyers need to engage, if not embrace, the realm of the possible opened up by technology.

How do you get this relationship started? As the definition states, "each entity must be flexible and adaptable." This correlates with probably one of the best takeaways from a former boss of mine, and a source of inspiration: To drive change, one must thrive in ambiguity. Be comfortable with the unknown and give it a try.

Luckily, you are not alone, and other members of this ecosystem can support you on that journey.

Colin Levy has been one of those members for some time. A key player in the legal ecosystem and, through the generous sharing of his experience, knowledge, and time, he has "impacted" other actors. He is one that isn't fazed by the unknown and is prone to collaboration.

I am lucky to count Colin as part of my community, the legal operations community, another growing key member of the legal ecosystem. And I am extremely honoured to acknowledge his contribution to helping us all on our journey.

Consider this book your starting point to demystify technology, make it more approachable and easily understood, and maybe even inspire you and others to engage and get out of their comfort zone. The potential is there, and technology could really become your best friend, helping you focus on the more strategic elements of your role and empowering you to do it even better—armed with more insights and data to make informed decisions.

Stéphanie Hamon, Norton Rose Fulbright

Further Reading

COMPLETE INTERVIEWS

1. https://www.colinslevy.com/blog/2017/11/13/legal-analytics/ (Kevin D. Ashley)

2. https://www.colinslevy.com/blog/2020/06/11/alma-asay/

3. https://www.colinslevy.com/blog/2018/06/04/professor-michael-l-bloom/

4. https://www.colinslevy.com/blog/2018/03/14/larry-bridgesmith/

5. https://www.colinslevy.com/blog/2019/04/06/kunoor-chopra/

6. https://www.colinslevy.com/blog/2018/02/26/mark-a-cohen-on-legal-innovation/

7. https://www.colinslevy.com/blog/2019/05/22/mark-deuitch/

8. https://www.colinslevy.com/blog/2018/03/21/ron-friedmann/

9. https://www.colinslevy.com/blog/2017/12/04/an-interview-with-jordan-furlong/

10. https://www.colinslevy.com/blog/2018/06/18/jordan-galvin/

11. https://www.colinslevy.com/blog/2020/09/16/carlos-gamez/

12. https://www.colinslevy.com/blog/2020/04/05/marlene-gebauer/

13. https://www.colinslevy.com/blog/2019/06/18/nir-golan/

14. https://www.colinslevy.com/blog/2018/02/14/a-few-words-from-kenneth-a-grady/

15. https://www.colinslevy.com/blog/2019/09/03/susan-hackett/

16. https://www.colinslevy.com/blog/2020/10/14/aaron-kotok/

17. https://www.colinslevy.com/blog/2020/03/14/catherine-krow/

18. https://www.colinslevy.com/blog/2018/03/07/josh-kubicki/

19. https://www.colinslevy.com/blog/2018/03/12/dan-linna/

20. https://www.colinslevy.com/blog/2018/04/16/cat-moon/

21. https://www.colinslevy.com/blog/2020/09/30/jack-newton/

22. https://www.colinslevy.com/blog/2020/03/01/quddus-pourshafie/

23. https://www.colinslevy.com/blog/2020/05/14/kenny-robertson/

24. https://www.colinslevy.com/blog/2019/06/30/ed-sohn/

25. https://www.colinslevy.com/blog/2019/12/08/quinten-steenhuis/

26. https://www.colinslevy.com/blog/2018/02/05/a-chat-with-bjarne-tellmann/

SUGGESTED BOOKS BY CATEGORY

Legal Innovation or Legal Technology

1. Bassli, Lucy Endel. *The Simple Guide to Legal Innovation: Basics Every Lawyer Should Know.* Chicago: American Bar Association, 2020.

2. Kennedy, Dennis M. *Successful Innovation Outcomes in Law: A Practical Guide for Law Firms, Law Departments and Other Legal Organizations.* Bowker Identification Services, 2019.

3. Kennedy, Dennis M. and Thomas L. Mighell. *The Lawyer's Guide to Collaboration Tools and Technologies: Smart Ways to Work Together.* 2d ed. Chicago: ABA Law Practice Division, 2018.

4. Waisberg, Noah and Alexander Hudek. *AI for Lawyers: How Artificial Intelligence Is Adding Value, Amplifying Expertise, and Transforming Careers.* Hoboken, NJ: John Wiley & Sons, 2021.

5. Walker, Joshua. *On Legal AI.* Full Court Press, 2019.

6. Walters, Ed, ed. *Data-Driven Law: Data Analytics and the New Legal Services.* Boca Raton, FL: CRC Press of Taylor and Francis Group, 2019.

Process Improvement

1. Lambreth, Susan Raridon, and David A. Rueff, Jr. *The Power of Legal Project Management: A Practical Handbook*. Chicago: American Bar Association, 2021.

2. MacDonagh, Catherine Alman. *Lean Six Sigma for Law Firms*. Woking, Surrey, United Kingdom: Globe Law and Business, 2021.

General Books on Legal Technology or Law

1. Furlong, Jordan. *Law is a Buyer's Market: Building a Client-First Law Firm*. Law21 Press, 2017.

2. Kowalski, Mitch. *Avoiding Extinction: Reimagining Legal Services for the 21st Century*. Bloomington, IN: iUniverse, 2012.

3. Susskind, Richard. *Tomorrow's Lawyers: An Introduction to Your Future*. Oxford, United Kingdom: Oxford University Press, 2017.

4. Susskind, Richard, and Daniel Susskind. *Future of the Professions: How Technology Will Transform the Work of Human Experts*. Oxford, United Kingdom: Oxford University Press, 2022.

5. Tellmann, Bjarne P. *Building an Outstanding Legal Team: Battle-Tested Strategies from a General Counsel*. Woking, Surrey, United Kingdom: Globe Law and Business, 2017.

6. Whelan Jr., Mike. *Lawyer Forward: Finding Your Place in the Future of Law*. 2019.

WEBSITES OF INTEREST

1. https://www.lawnext.com/

2. https://www.colinslevy.com/

3. https://www.denniskennedy.com/

4. https://prismlegal.com/

5. https://www.artificiallawyer.com/

Biographies

Alma Asay is a legal technology expert and trusted advisor to Litera Microsystems clients, helping them bring innovative ways of thinking and practice to life. Before joining Litera, Alma was the chief innovation officer, Legal Solutions, at Integreon Discovery Solutions, a leading global provider of alternative legal services. Alma joined Integreon as part of its acquisition of her litigation management software business, Allegory Law, where she was founder and CEO. Allegory Law is a platform offered in the cloud and on-premises that automates everyday litigation tasks and connects the people, facts, and evidence that litigation teams need to build their winning story in a central, secure place.

Jason Barnwell leads Microsoft's Legal Business, Operations, and Strategy team. He is also an innovator, a software developer, and a thought leader. Jason's professional focus is leading innovation efforts for Microsoft's legal department. He is passionate about developing and commercializing technology and works to make the legal profession and industry a more diverse and inclusive place across every axis.

Josh Blandi founded UniCourt after a few years of running his first company, CountryWide Debt Relief, a high-volume, low-cost legal services model used by law firms to help consumers consolidate and eliminate their debt. The UniCourt platform uses sophisticated data-gathering techniques to collect court data from hundreds of state and federal courts across the United States.

Michael L. Bloom has "been curating spaces for students and professionals to make mistakes—and learn from them—since 2009." Michael founded and runs Praktio, a provider of interactive, online learning games and exercises for developing practical contracts skills and know-how. At the University of Michigan Law School, Michael was the founding director of the Transactional Lab & Clinic, an experiential program through which students work on transactional matters, under faculty supervision, for large, mature organizations around the world (*e.g.*, Pepsi, Aon, National Public Radio) and small, local organizations near the law school.

Larry Bridgesmith is adjunct professor of law at Vanderbilt University and a leading voice in the legal innovation space. He has more than 30 years of experience in the dispute resolution and innovation fields. He also co-founded LPM Alignment, which is the first approved training in the United States for the certification program of the International Institute for Legal Project Management.

Jeff Carr describes himself as a legal rebel. He has spent more than 30 years fighting for change within the legal industry, most recently as general counsel for several large companies, including Univar Solutions. Before this, and after retiring as general counsel of FMC in 2014, Jeff worked with Valorem Law, one of the earliest law firms to focus on making alternative fee arrangements the norm. Valorem served as the basis for ElevateNext, the law firm affiliate of the global law company, Elevate. When not pushing for change, Jeff is an active race car driver.

Kunoor Chopra has been involved in the legal services outsourcing industry since 2004, when she founded LawScribe, one of the pioneer companies in the industry. Her vision has always been to create a platform that provides customers with the best, most effective and efficient options to obtain and manage legal services. This means transforming the way legal services are delivered through technology and by providing customers with the right resources for service delivery, domain experts, process efficiencies, and visibility into the who, what, where, and how of the services being delivered.

Mark A. Cohen is the CEO of Legal Mosaic, a legal business consultancy that provides strategic advice to corporate legal departments, law firms, legal service providers, legal networks, entrepreneurs, and law schools. He is frequently engaged as a keynote speaker and has spoken and consulted throughout North America, Europe, Asia, South America, Africa, and Australia. Mark is also a co-founder and executive chairman of the Digital Legal Exchange, a unique, global, not-for-profit organization created to teach, apply, and scale digital principles to the legal function.

Dan Currell is an experienced lawyer and management consultant, legal innovation leader, and currently serves as senior advisor within the Office of Finance and Operations at the U.S. Department of Education.

Mark Deuitch is an entrepreneur and the founder of two web-based start-ups, PeopleClaim and Rhubarb (an online consensus decision and dispute resolution community). Mark is devoted to solving "societal issues that are not sufficiently resolved by the existing system."

Gary Doernhoefer served as the first general counsel for the travel website, Orbitz, co-founded and served as general counsel for Accertify, Inc. (now a wholly owned subsidiary of American Express), and served as vice president and general counsel through the launch and initial capitalization of Journera, a travel industry technology start-up company. Gary served for three years as general counsel for the International Air Transport Association, the global trade association for the world's airline industry. After three decades of experience managing legal issues and disputes in a wide variety of contexts and helping to launch three start-up companies, Gary became the founder and managing director of ADR Notable, a leading company in the alternative dispute resolution sector.

Daniel Farris is a former software engineer and network administrator, a founder of the legal technology firm, Proxy, and a technology and intellectual property attorney.

Ron Friedmann is a well-known lawyer and thought leader in the legal innovation space with more than 20 years' experience in the legal field. Ron is an expert in law practice management, outsourcing, knowledge management, contract management, e-discovery, legal marketing, and technology for lawyers.

Jordan Furlong is a leading analyst of the global legal market, forecaster of its future development, and thought leader in the area of legal innovation. Jordan is a frequent speaker and has spoken at events held by a variety of law firms and lawyers' organizations, legal regulators, and many others throughout North America, Europe, and Australia. Jordan is also the author of the highly regarded book, *Law Is a Buyer's Market.*

Jordan Galvin is a true innovator and someone who welcomes change and disruption. She currently is knowledge management resources lead at Mayer Brown and was previously fellow and innovation counsel at the LegalRnD Program of the Center for Legal Services Innovation at Michigan State University College of Law.

Carlos Gamez is a leading legal thinker and legal innovator. He has been leading legal innovation initiatives at Thomson Reuters for the past several years, as part of the legal business, Thomson Reuters Labs, and most recently within a dedicated legal technology innovation team. Over time, he has worked on and delivered more than 50 projects in partnership with stakeholders across the enterprise, as well as externally with customers, start-ups, academic institutions, and industry forums. Carlos also has been involved with helping to define and refine the innovation and emerging technology strategy for law firms and corporate counsel.

Dennis Garcia is an assistant general counsel for Microsoft and leads the legal support function to Microsoft's U.S. Enterprise Commercial team—a group of more than 2,000 sales, marketing, technical, and services professionals that manages Microsoft's largest commercial business. Dennis has practiced at the intersection of law, technology and business for more than 20 years to drive positive impact for three technology leaders: Microsoft, Accenture, and IBM. Dennis is also active on social media as a technology evangelist and legal industry thought leader. He writes an award-winning blog, *In-House Consigliere*, about the practice of law.

Heidi K. Gardner, PhD, is a Distinguished Fellow at Harvard Law School and faculty chair of the school's Accelerated Leadership Program, Smart Collaboration Masterclass and other programs. Previously, she was a professor at Harvard Business School. Heidi is co-founder of Gardner & Co., a research/advisory firm.

Marlene Gebauer is global director of strategic legal insights at Greenberg Traurig, LLP, and serves as host of the popular *The Geek in Review* podcast.

Gerald Glover III is a lawyer and legal technologist serving as client relations & inclusion senior manager for Orrick, Herrington & Sutcliffe LLP.

Nir Golan is an innovative attorney and legal operations professional focused on advising and working with multinational organizations. Nir is a strong believer that legal work is about problem solving, creating solutions, and delivering business outcomes. He thrives on supporting, motivating, and empowering strong, collaborative, and diverse teams.

Raj Goyle is CEO and co-founder of Bodhala, the market leader in legal business intelligence.

Kenneth A. Grady works on transforming the legal industry, using his experiences as a general counsel, law firm partner, CEO of a law firm subsidiary, legal industry consultant, and law college adjunct professor and research fellow. Ken focuses on lawyers, law firms, and law companies becoming innovative, efficient, and affordable legal service providers. He is able to see things from the perspective of clients, but with the insights of the service provider. Ken has spoken around the world at major conferences, law department retreats, seminars, and in-house workshops on how to participate and succeed in transforming the legal industry.

Susan Hackett is a powerful voice within the legal profession, especially with regard to change and transformation within the legal industry. She currently is CEO of Legal Executive Leadership, LLC, which is a recognized leader in building smarter legal practices, and has more than three decades of experience helping law departments deliver value and improve the way they work. She helps her clients change behaviors, improve operational processes, drive demonstrable client results, and move confidently from traditional practice toward legal executive leadership.

Stéphanie Hamon is the head of Legal Operations Consulting at Norton Rose Fulbright and a former managing director, head of External Engagement, Legal for Barclays. She has extensive experience setting and delivering commercial and business management strategies for in-house legal departments. Hamon led the Barclays team that was named "Legal operations team of the year" at the 2019 UK Legal 500 Awards.

Bill Henderson is a long-time educator and leader in innovative legal education. He heads the Institute for the Future of Law Practice.

Daniel Katz is a scientist, technologist, and professor who applies an innovative polytechnic approach to teaching law with the aim of helping to create lawyers who can meet today's biggest societal challenges. His scholarship and his teaching integrate science, technology, engineering, and mathematics. Daniel is well-known for his work in legal informatics, which the American Library Association defines as being "the study of the structure and properties of information, as well as the application of technology to the organization, storage, retrieval, and dissemination of information."

Dennis Kennedy is well-known for promoting innovation and the use of technology in law practice. He is an information technology and digital transformation lawyer. He helps forward-looking legal organizations improve their innovation efforts. Dennis is also an innovation consultant, author, and speaker who is well-known for understanding underlying technologies and platforms while being easy to work with, responsive to global clients, and focused on real-world results.

Mitch Kowalski is a leader in the legal innovation space. He has spent more than 25 years in a variety of roles in the legal space, as a lawyer, writer, and professor, and is the author of the critically acclaimed books, *Avoiding Extinction: Reimagining Legal Services for the 21st Century* and *The Great Legal Reformation: Notes From the Field.*

Catherine Krow is the founder of Digitory Legal, an award-winning cost analytics platform focused on bringing data-driven pricing and cost prediction to law. Before founding Digitory Legal, Catherine practiced law at top-tier firms for 17 years, first at Simpson, Thacher & Bartlett, LLP, and then at Orrick, where she was a litigation partner. Catherine is also a frequent speaker and recognized thought leader on legal technology, spend management, and the use of artificial intelligence and data in law.

David Lat is the founder of the news website, *Above the Law.* He clerked for Judge Diarmuid F. O'Scannlain of the Ninth Circuit after law school, then spent some time as a litigator in New York, followed by a stint at the Office of the U.S. Attorney for the district of New Jersey. He started a blog that was well-received and soon left the U.S. Attorney's office to be a full-time blogger.

Marc Lauritsen is president of Capstone Practice Systems. Capstone advises, trains, and builds systems for top law firms and departments, as well as many nonprofit organizations. Marc has served as a poverty lawyer, taught in and directed the clinical program at Harvard Law School, done path-breaking work on document automation and artificial intelligence, and has been an executive in several startups. Marc is a leader in international law and technology organizations, a fellow of the College of Law Practice Management, and past co-chair of the American Bar Association's eLawyering Task Force.

Peter Lederer has spent 70 years within the legal industry and has served as a partner of a major law firm and as general counsel of a global corporation. He is well-known as a forward-thinking teacher, leader, and lawyer.

Dan Linna, a leading legal thinker, is professor of law in residence and the director of the LegalRnD Program of the Center for Legal Services Innovation at Michigan State University College of Law. He is very well-known for his groundbreaking expertise in the area of "Lean" thinking as applied to the delivery of legal services, especially his Legal Innovation Services Index.

Olga V. Mack is CEO of Parley Pro, a modern, collaborative, and intuitive contract management platform that has pioneered online negotiation technology. She is also an award-winning general counsel, operations professional, start-up advisor, public speaker, adjunct professor, and entrepreneur. Olga co-founded SunLaw, an organization dedicated to preparing female in-house attorneys to become general counsel and legal leaders, and WISE to help female law firm partners become rainmakers. Olga is passionate about disruptive technologies such as blockchain and artificial intelligence. She served as vice president of strategy at Quantstamp (YC W18), the first decentralized security auditing blockchain platform. She also co-authored *Fundamentals of Smart Contract Security* and wrote *Blockchain Business Models*.

Nehal Madhani was a practicing attorney at an internationally known law firm when he was inspired to make legal practice more efficient. He taught himself programming and founded Alt Legal, a company whose cloud-based trademark docketing software helps legal professionals prepare and manage hundreds of thousands of trademark filings and deadlines daily. Nehal speaks regularly about the intersection of legal practice and technology to bar associations and at legal conferences, including the New York County Lawyers Association, the New York State Bar Association, the Florida Bar, and the annual Clio Cloud Conference. He has been profiled in *Inc.* magazine, *Bloomberg News*, and on *Above the Law* and *Attorney at Work* websites.

Thabo Magubane is a legal tech thought leader and chief of growth for Legal Connection, a legal tech company.

Maya Markovich has a passion for transforming the practice of law. As head of product for Nextlaw Labs, Maya is currently focused on building momentum for innovation within the ecosystem of Dentons, the largest law firm in the world, and across the industry.

Eli Mattern is a lawyer and a leading legal technology entrepreneur. She practiced law as a legal aid attorney for five years before making the switch to legal technology and legal start-ups. She co-founded and is CEO of SavvySuit, which builds access to justice software and products for the private bar.

Varun Mehta is the CEO of Factor, a leader in complex legal work at scale. Factor serves more than 50 of the Fortune 500/FTSE 100 companies, combining the legal skill, market know-how, and expertise of traditional law with the process efficiency, technology, and data orientation of "New Law." A long-time problem-solver and biomedical engineer by training, Varun is a trusted advisor to general counsel and legal operations leaders within global organizations. His efforts have helped legal departments innovate, transformed how legal work is delivered, and generated value across the legal landscape.

Dorna Moini, a former litigator at Sidley Austin, is the CEO and co-founder of Documate, a platform for building document automation and client-facing legal applications. Her pro bono practice at Sidley Austin involved working with legal aid organizations to build a web application to allow domestic violence survivors to complete and file their paperwork, which led to the idea for Documate. Dorna is on the Legal Services Corporation Emerging Leaders Council and is a member of the Advisory Board of the Legal Aid Foundation of Los Angeles. She was named an American Bar Association Legal Rebel and a Fastcase 50 honoree. She also teaches the Legal Innovations Lab at USC Gould School of Law.

Cat Moon is director of innovation design in the Program of Law and Innovation (PoLI) and lecturer in law at Vanderbilt University Law School, where she teaches law students critical 21st-century lawyering skills. Cat also works with colleagues to develop innovative curriculum offerings that are responsive to the demands of a rapidly evolving legal profession. In addition, as director of the PoLI Institute at Vanderbilt Law, she helps lawyers gain these same critical innovation leadership skills through intensive, interactive courses presented at Vanderbilt's innovation hub, the Wond'ry.

Jack Newton is a name familiar to many with an interest in legal technology. He is the forward-thinking CEO and founder of Clio, a legal technology company focused on making technologies to help lawyers manage legal matters and client relationships.

Mary O'Carroll is co-founder of the Corporate Legal Operations Consortium and was one of the first to make the idea of, and need for, legal operations well known.

Kimball Parker is the founder of SixFifty, director of the Legal Design Clinic at Brigham Young University, and a former attorney who founded the innovation subsidiary of the law firm, Parsons Behle & Latimer. His passion and dedication to making the legal system more accessible and less costly is evident in all that he has achieved.

Quddus Pourshafie is director at NFTUX and an educator and legal technology founder who developed what he calls the Future Framework for Legal Practice.

Kenny Robertson is head of the Outsourcing, Technology & Intellectual Property legal team at Royal Bank of Scotland. He has led some of the largest technology outsourcing projects in the United Kingdom and is additionally responsible for the bank's roll out and adoption of legal technology.

Nelson Rosario is an attorney licensed to practice in Illinois and has worked with clients in a range of areas, including artificial intelligence, cryptocurrency, blockchain, and smart contracts; financial technologies; business methods; trading systems; telemedicine; network and internet communication; and navigation and routing. Nelson has served as an adjunct professor at the Chicago-Kent College of Law at the Illinois Institute of Technology, where he has taught classes on blockchain, cryptocurrency, and the law and international technology, artificial intelligence, and digital privacy. He has given numerous talks on emerging technologies and the legal considerations surrounding them.

Quinten Steenhuis, senior housing attorney and network administrator for Greater Boston Legal Services, is an advocate of using technology to reduce the need for legal aid clients to come to the office. He is the creator of Massachusetts Defense for Eviction, which assists clients with the forms needed for court and reminds them of court dates automatically.

Alex Su is a leader in the use of social media within the legal space. Although he started posting about legal technology, he is now well-known for his humorous memes making fun of lawyers and lawyers' behavior.

Bjarne P. Tellmann is general counsel of the health solutions company, Haleon, and former senior vice president and general counsel at GSK Consumer Healthcare.

Gabriel H. Teninbaum is currently serving as assistant dean of Innovation, Strategic Initiatives and Distance Education, at Suffolk University Law School.

Richard Tromans is the founder and editor of the popular legal technology website, *Artificial Lawyer*. He is also the founder of Tromans Consulting, a London-based consulting company for legal service providers and law firms. He is quoted frequently at conferences and law firm events, especially on the topics of artificial intelligence and smart contracts.

Akshay Verma is former head of legal operations for Meta and current head of legal operations for Coinbase.

Joshua Walker is a leading expert on AI in law and is the author of *On Legal AI* published by Full Court Press.

Tunji Williams is a dreamer, intrapreneur, technologist, and mergers and acquisitions attorney who is developing teams and strategies to help revolutionize deal process technology and service delivery for corporate transactions, and beyond.

COLIN S. LEVY
LEGAL TECHNOLOGY MAVEN

Visit www.colinslevy.com and sign up to stay abreast of the most current information in the legal tech ecosystem. You'll get access to exclusive interviews with leaders in the legal technology space. Discover invaluable insights, read inspiring stories, enjoy *insider-only* video content, and learn about integrating legal tech into the practice of law.

Whether you are just starting out in the legal industry or are a seasoned professional looking to stay up to date with the latest trends, get in on the best reporting from the front line of legal technology.

Index

Figures and notes are indicated by f and n following the page numbers.

A

Made in the USA
Middletown, DE
15 October 2023

40622213R00136